EQ5 DRAWING

Exercises in Block Design by Patti R. Anderson

The Electric Quilt Company
419 Gould Street, Suite 2
Bowling Green, OH 43402

The Electric Quilt Company
419 Gould Street, Suite 2
Bowling Green, OH 43402-3047
419-352-1134
E-mail: sales@electricquilt.com
Web site: www.electricquilt.com

Credits

Editors:	Jill Badenhop, Penny McMorris, Elena Landa, Ashley Nelson, Sharon Chase
Cover Design:	Jill Badenhop
Book Design:	Tracey Budden
Technical Help:	Ann Rutter

Block designs shown on front cover designed by Patti R. Anderson.

EQ5 Drawing

Acknowledgements

My sincerest thanks go to:

• All the folks of the **Electric Quilt Company**. Extra special thanks go to **Dean Neumann, Penny McMorris, Ann Rutter** (who was my contact person and very diplomatic sounding board), **Jill Badenhop, Tracey Budden, Elena Landa, Ashley Nelson**, and **Sharon Chase**. You are a great bunch of people to work with and all your hard work makes me look good!

• **Fran Gonzalez**, who called me on the phone when she found out I was doing this book and welcomed me to the world of "crazy EQ writers."

• **Barb Vlack**, who was always able to get my creative juices going with a good drawing challenge.

• **Carol Miller**, Dean of Quilt University (www.quiltuniversity.com), who asked me to join the online faculty of QU and teach the feature specific and advanced level EQ classes.

• **Members of the Info-EQ mailing list** – I would not be writing this book if it were not for you, in fact...*this book really is for you!*

• **Gilmer County Arts & Heritage Council of West Virginia** for awarding me a grant with which I was able to purchase my first Electric Quilt software. It was awarded to me to help in the pursuit of my quilting art. I never dreamed where it would take me!

• My husband, **Robert M. Anderson**, who is not only my closest friend and loving companion, but my biggest fan club. He's my geometry teacher when I can't even describe what I am trying to do, and he is the epitome of patience when it comes to dealing with a spouse who is obsessed with quilting.

• My daughters, **Naomi** and **Bethany Anderson**, for putting up with a mom who many times they would find glued to the computer keyboard.

• And in honor of my mom, **Mildred Susan Rader Cottrell**, who passed away during the time I was writing this book. She was a person who dedicated her life to loving her family and her Maker and passed that gift onto the next generation. My mom taught me to sew "real good" and taught me not to give up until I had the project the way it was supposed to be. Mom, you were one very special and beautiful lady. I miss you.

Table of Contents

EQ5 Drawing

Introduction

I like to think of EQ5 as being like a well-stocked kitchen. We have all the ingredients and tools we need to create an endless supply of blocks. If we are pressed for time, we can have instant blocks from the thousands given to us in the Block Libraries. If that's not enough, we can use a block from the library as a starter ingredient for a new block. And if we are the adventurous type quilt chef, we can create our own great blocks from scratch. With EQ5 we can cook up a different block *at least* three times a day and then some!

About this book...

With the exception of a suggestion or two for a quilt layout, this entire book takes place on the Block Worktable. This book is all about drawing blocks! Think of the exercises in this book as a collection of recipes for tasty dishes you have always wanted to try. You not only get a picture of every block in the book, but you also get illustrated step-by-step instructions for creating them! Although it's designed progressively, feel free to flip through the book, choose a block and draw it.

Warning! You need to come to the kitchen...or rather to the computer, with some basic training behind you. This book does not tell you how to preheat the oven or how to test to see if your cake is done, nor does it cover how to open and save project files or what the difference is between EasyDraw™ and PatchDraw. In other words...I am assuming you will have worked through the **EQ5 Getting Started** manual and will have read through at least most of the **EQ5 Design Cookbook** (especially Chapter 7 on Blocks). Working through Fran Gonzalez's book, **EQ5 Simplified**, will equip you even more.

Keep the above books on hand in case you need to refer to something I assume you already know. I should mention that this book does not instruct you to color your new blocks. I used the book space to squeeze in as many blocks as possible, so I left out coloring. However, I think you will not be able to resist coloring the blocks anyway, so I really didn't need to tell you, did I? Be sure you know all about saving blocks in the User Libraries (pages 14 – 17.) I definitely think you will want to save your newly drawn blocks in the User Library. What it all boils down to is this...you are comfortable and familiar with the basics of EQ5 and now you are anxious to cook up some really cool blocks on your own!

The exercises in the first chapter will get you warmed up to using to the five basic drawing tools and the wide array of drawing aids available in EQ5. In the second chapter, you will need to don your chef's hat. We'll turn on the Advanced Drawing features and you will be amazed at the block potential as you learn to work with the gourmet tools of EQ5. The remainder of the book is all desserts! Most of the blocks in the last two chapters are there because *you* asked if it was possible. The answer is, yes!

One of the hardest parts of doing this book was deciding which blocks to include. Many are blocks *you* have asked me how to draw (lots of eight-pointed stars, for example), some are blocks popular with quilters everywhere. Other blocks are from my own imagination — never seen before this book — given to you to show you how to stretch *your* drawing imagination. All of these blocks will teach you something as you go through the exercises.

EQ5 Drawing

You will notice I strive for accuracy as much as possible in drawing a block. I'm really not that particular; I just believe that if it's possible to achieve it, why not try? My goal is to teach you to use EQ5's tools creatively.

Do you like to create your own recipes? Time and time again I have made new discoveries with this software just by experimenting. I hope this book encourages you to do the same. I've given you lots of variations to try at the end of lessons. I hope these will inspire you to take what you have learned in the exercise one step further and beyond. Come join me in my EQ5 kitchen and we'll whip up some fantastic blocks together…

Patti R. Anderson

Chapter 1 Color Illustrations

1

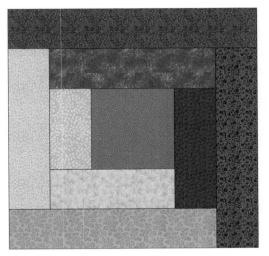

Log Cabin
Page 8

Double Irish Chain
Page 10

Sawtooth Star
Page 12

New York
Page 22

1

Simple Paper Piecing
Page 24

Delectable Mountains
Page 26

Border & Setting Triangles
Page 30

LeMoyne Star
Page 36

Hunter's Star
Page 38

Nosegay
Page 40

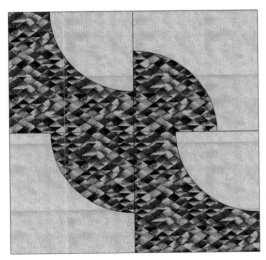

Drunkard's Path
Page 42

1930's Posy
Page 45

1

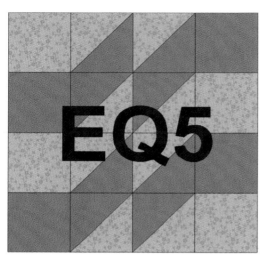

Appliqué Letters
Page 54

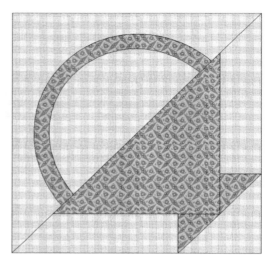

Flower Basket
Page 60

Tree of Life
Page 64

Basic Block Drawing

Chapter 1

Chapter 1 Overview

All the drawing exercises in this chapter use only the basic drawing tools in EasyDraw™ and PatchDraw. Each exercise is designed to teach and emphasize a particular aspect of drawing in EQ5, with the goal in mind for you to learn to feel comfortable drawing from scratch. Best of all, you will be learning these basics while drawing blocks that are popular and have earned the status of favorite quilt blocks.

You will also learn to make use of the many drawing aids and special menus that are available in EQ5...like the graph paper lines, guidelines, the Symmetry pop-up menu, the Edit Line/Arc pop-up menu...just to name a few!

Although you may find it helpful to work through the exercises in the order they appear, do not feel that you are bound by that fact. If you jump ahead and get stuck, go back and work through the previous exercises and see if it helps. At the end of most of the exercises, I have included several variations of the block for you to try on your own using the skills you have learned. There are plenty of things to keep you busy, so work through them at your own pace and enjoy. And hey, if the exercises and variations inspire you to go off on a drawing tangent of your own – go for it! Think of the exercises in this chapter as low-impact exercises – absolutely nothing strenuous, but doing them will get you in shape for the fun drawing yet to come!

Drawing a Log Cabin Block

Color block
on page 1*

Let's create a simple Log Cabin block and learn how to use the graph paper lines in EQ5 to make it easy to draw too!

1   On the WORKTABLE menu, click Work on Block.

2   On the BLOCK menu, point to New Block, click EasyDraw™.

3   Click on the BLOCK menu again, click Drawing Board Setup.

4   On the General tab, in Snap to Grid Points, type 24 in both the Horizontal and Vertical division boxes.

5   On the General tab, in Block Size, type 6 in both the Horizontal and Vertical boxes.

6   On the Graph Paper tab, in Number of Divisions, type 6 in both the Horizontal and Vertical boxes.

7   Also on the Graph Paper tab, in Options, click the down arrow on the Style box and select Graph paper lines.

8   Click OK. The graph paper lines will be visible on the drawing board now.

✎ Tip

- **Like real graph paper, the graph paper lines in EQ5 are a visual aid to help you draw your block. If the graph paper divisions are set to match your Snap to Grid Points or your Block Size, it will make drawing a block from scratch much easier. For a Log Cabin block in particular, they are the visual aid to help you draw your logs.**

9   Click on the Line tool.

10   Draw a horizontal line from left to right across the block beginning 1.00" down from the top. If the Rulers are not showing on the top and left side of the drawing board, click on the VIEW menu and click to check Rulers. The graph paper lines show you exactly where to draw!

Step 1

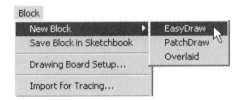

Step 2

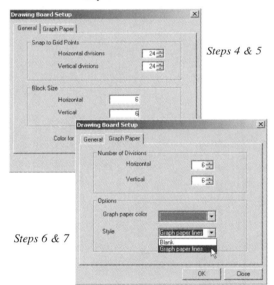

Steps 4 & 5

Steps 6 & 7

Step 9
Line Tool

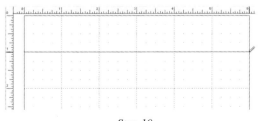

Step 10

1

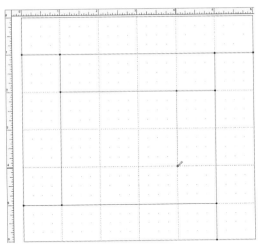

Step 14

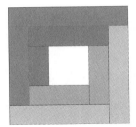

Step 15
Save in Sketchbook

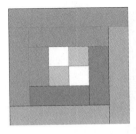

Completed
Log Cabin Block

Try these variations of the Log Cabin block

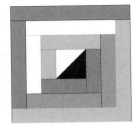

This is the same block as in the first exercise, but lines were added to make a four patch in the center.

This block uses 24 x 24 snap to grid points, but the logs are 0.75". Hint: Change the block size and the graph paper divisions to 8 x 8.

11 Draw a vertical line to the bottom of the block beginning at the first drawn line and 1.00" from the right side of the block.

12 Draw a horizontal line from right to left across the block beginning at the second drawn line and 1.00" from the bottom of the block.

13 Draw a vertical line beginning at the third drawn line and 1.00" from the left side of the block and ending at the first drawn line.

14 Drawing in a clockwise direction, draw four more lines. Begin each new line at the previously drawn line, spacing them 1.00" from the first round of logs, and leaving a 2.00" square in the center of the block.

15 Click on the Save in Sketchbook button to save your block

Imagine if you had to draw this block without the aid of the graph paper lines – it would not be so easy! Graph paper lines are just one of the drawing aids that EQ provides for us. Once you learn how to make them work for you, you will use them often.

↘ Tip ─────────────

- **It is much easier to draw a Log Cabin block going from the outside of the block to the inside. Although it doesn't matter on which side of the block you draw the first line, it is important to always go in one direction around the block - either clockwise or counterclockwise.**

- **If you know the size block you want, you can draw the center square of a Log Cabin block first. Once you draw the center square, divide the remaining space equally to determine how wide to draw your "logs." Depending on the width of your logs, you may need to adjust the Snap to Grid points and the Graph Paper lines.**

Drawing a Double Irish Chain Block

Color block on page 1

You can use the Grid tool to divide your block or areas of your block into evenly divided patches. Let's try it out while making a traditional Irish Chain block.

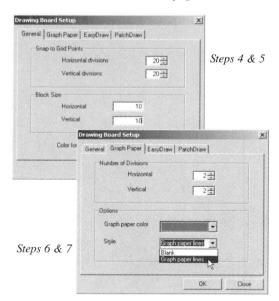

Steps 4 & 5

1   On the WORKTABLE menu, click Work on Block.

2   On the BLOCK menu, point to New Block, click EasyDraw™.

3   Click on the BLOCK menu again, click Drawing Board Setup.

4   On the General tab, in Snap to Grid Points, type 20 in both the Horizontal and Vertical division boxes.

Steps 6 & 7

5   Also on the General tab, in Block Size, type 10 in both the Horizontal and Vertical boxes.

6   On the Graph Paper tab, in Number of Divisions, type 2 in both the Horizontal and Vertical boxes.

7   Also on the Graph Paper tab, in Options, click the down arrow on the Style box and select Graph paper lines.

Step 9
Line Tool

8   Click OK. The graph paper lines will be visible on the drawing board now dividing the block into four equal sections.

9   Click on the Line tool.

10   Following the graph paper lines, draw a horizontal and vertical line in the center of the block to divide the block into a four patch.

Step 10

11   Click on the Grid tool, clicking on the small black square in the lower left corner on the button to bring up the Grid Setup box.

Step 11
Grid Tool

12   In the Grid Setup box, click the arrow buttons to change the number to 5 for both the Columns and Rows.

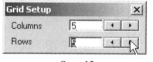

Step 12

1

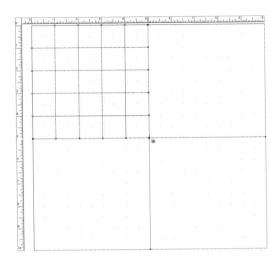

Step 13

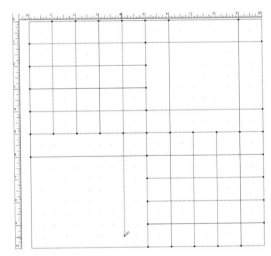

Step 16

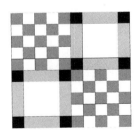

*Completed Double
Irish Chain Block*

13 Notice that the cursor has changed to a crosshair with a grid. Point the crosshair center on the upper-left corner of the block and drag the grid diagonally to the center point of the block and release the mouse. A 5 x 5 grid is now placed in the upper-left quadrant of the block.

Tip
- When placing your grid on the block, you need to drag the cursor diagonally. If you make a mistake or release the mouse button too soon, use CTRL+Z to undo your drawing immediately, or on the EDIT menu click Undo. Then try again.

14 Still using the Grid tool, point the cursor at the center of the block and drag the grid diagonally to the bottom-right corner of the block. A 5 x 5 grid is now placed in the lower right quadrant of the block.

15 Click on the Line tool.

16 In each of the remaining two quadrants of the block, draw four lines (two horizontal and two vertical) 1.00" away from the grids and from the edge of the block. This creates a 3.00" framed square in these remaining quadrants and completes the Double Irish Chain block.

17 Click on the Save in Sketchbook button to save your block.

Tip
- To have a grid that is made up of perfect squares, the number of columns and rows in Grid Setup must divide evenly into the horizontal and vertical Snap to Grid points in the Drawing Board Setup. You can easily see the Snap points on the Block Worktable by looking at the Status bar on the lower-right of the worktable screen.
- The Grid Setup box will remain open until you click on the X to close it, or until you click on another drawing tool.

Drawing a Sawtooth Star Block

Color block on page 1

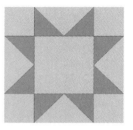

This very popular star block has been around since the early 1800's. It can easily be drawn on a 4 x 4 grid, even though it's not technically a Four Patch block.

1 On the WORKTABLE menu, click Work on Block.

2 On the BLOCK menu, point to New Block, click EasyDraw™.

3 Click on the BLOCK menu again, click Drawing Board Setup.

4 On the General tab, in Snap to Grid Points, type 24 in both the Horizontal and Vertical division boxes.

5 Also on the General tab, in Block Size, type 6 in both the Horizontal and Vertical boxes.

6 On the Graph Paper tab, in Number of Divisions, type 4 in both the Horizontal and Vertical boxes.

7 Also on the Graph Paper tab, in Options, click the down arrow on the Style box and select Graph paper lines.

8 Click OK. The graph paper lines will be visible on the drawing board now.

Sawtooth Star Block

Step 1

Step 3

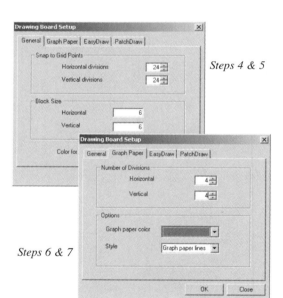

Steps 4 & 5

Steps 6 & 7

Step 9
Line Tool

9 Click on the Line tool.

10 Draw two horizontal lines across the block, one line at 1.50" and one line at 4.50".

11 Draw two vertical lines from the top to the bottom of the block, one line at 1.50" and one line at 4.50".

12 On the left and right sides, and on the top and bottom of the block, draw two 45° diagonal lines between the drawn lines, beginning at the outside of the block and ending at the center point of the drawn lines.

Notice how helpful the graph paper lines are by showing you exactly where the center line crosses the drawn lines.

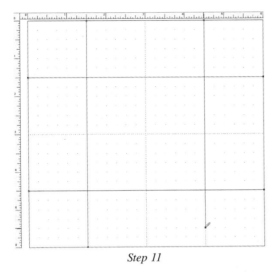

Step 11

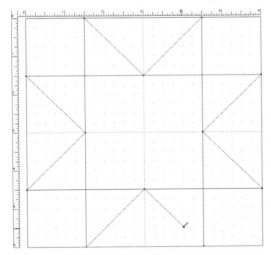

Step 12

13 Click on the Save in Sketchbook button to save your block.

Step 13
Save in Sketchbook

If you plan to use this block in future quilts or block designs, keep reading to learn how to save it in your User Library. (Hint: We will be using this block later in the book!)

Saving Blocks in the User Libraries

If you want your blocks available to use in *any* project, save them in the library (as well as in your project).

1 Start with a block on the screen that you want to save in the Block Library. Click the Save in Sketchbook button.

2 On the LIBRARIES menu, click Add Blocks. You will see a Block Libraries book with a User Libraries book under it.

✎ **Tip** ────────────

• **If you do not see the User Libraries book, double-click the Block Libraries book to open it.**

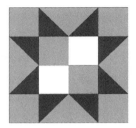

Completed Sawtooth Block   *Variation 1*

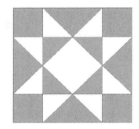

Variation 2   *Variation 3*

Step 2

Tip – Double-click the Block Libraries book to open the User Libraries book.

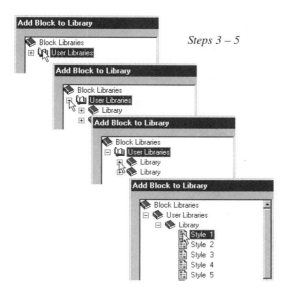

Steps 3 – 5

Steps 6 & 7

3 Click User Libraries, then click its +

4 Click the + sign next to a Library book appears. You will now see Style pages. These pages are empty, waiting to be fill with blocks.

5 Click any style page to select that style. Under "Current Library Style," you will see "No blocks to display" unless you previously added blocks to this style.

6 Under "Block Sketchbook," click the tab that contains the designs you want to add to your Block Library.

7 Now that you are on the correct tab, click the block you want to add to the library. (If you do not see your block, click, hold, and drag the slider bar under the Block Sketchbook to view all of the blocks.)

8 Click Copy. You will now see your block under Current Library Style.

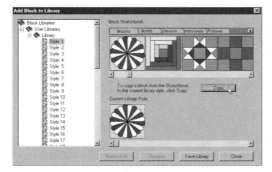

Step 8

9 Click the Save Library button, to save your changes to that style. A message saying, "Your blocks have been saved in the library!" will appear. Click OK.

10 Continue copying as many blocks from their tabs in the Block Sketchbook to the style(s) of your libraries. Remember to save the style before switching to another style.

11 Click Close when you are finished. (If you did not save your library style, you will receive the message "You have changed the current library style. Do you want to save the library and make your changes permanent?" Click the Yes button.)

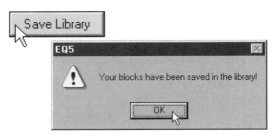

Step 9

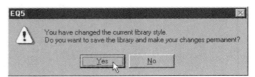

Step 11

Tip ───────────────

• **You cannot put two copies of the same block under one style. You will receive a message, "This block is already in the current library style!"**

• **If the blocks you save have prints in them, you will save the blocks, not the prints. When you get the blocks from the library, just recolor the blocks.**

1

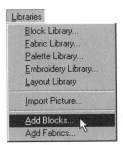

Step 1

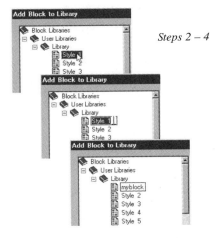

Steps 2 – 4

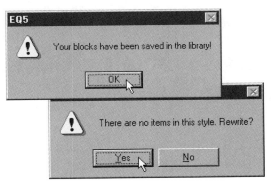

Step 5

Renaming Library Styles

1 On the LIBRARIES menu, click Add Blocks.

2 Click a Style. The name will become highlighted.

3 Click the Style name again. A box will form around it.

4 Type your new name (up to 32 characters). The old name disappears as you type.

5 Click Save Library.

If the style *has* blocks in it there will be a message saying, "Your blocks have been saved in the library!" You've saved your new library name.
If the style *does not have* blocks in it there will be a message saying, "There are no items in this style. Rewrite?" Click Yes. Now you will receive a message saying, "Your blocks have been saved in the library!" You've saved your new library name.

6 Click Close when you are finished renaming the library and style.

Tip

• If you name your style a word that would alphabetically fall behind the word "Style," look for it under all the other Style names. If you name your style "Teddy Bears," for example, you'll need to scroll to the bottom of the list, beneath the last style, to find it.

Finding the Secret Patch Code

Four patch, five patch, seven patch, nine patch... which is it? Once you figure this out, drawing a traditional pieced quilt block with EasyDraw™ is a snap!

Using EasyDraw™ to draw a pieced block is much like working with graph paper, only we use a mouse instead of a pencil, and our rulers are right there on the drawing board. The biggest advantage of EQ5 over paper and pencil is that we can print our blocks any size we want. With a click of the mouse we can print templates, foundation patterns, rotary cutting charts, or just print the block by itself. Even though we might draw our blocks a certain size, we don't necessarily need to print them that size.

Most traditional pieced blocks can be drafted on a square grid. However, when we call a block a four patch for example, we are referring to the units by which the block is sewn together, and that's not the same as the grid needed to draw the block. To set our Snap to Grid points correctly, we need to visualize a grid of squares superimposed over the block. These virtual divisions are the key to setting up the snap points in EasyDraw™. I call these divisions the **secret patch code**.

However, some blocks do not divide evenly into a square grid. Blocks like eight-point stars, blocks with curves, hexagons, and others have their own special secret patch code. Most can still be drawn in EasyDraw™ once you learn the secret. We'll talk about some of these later in the book.

Cracking the Code

Sorry, but there is no magic formula we can use to calculate the secret patch code. However, just like cracking a real code, we can learn to do it by observation, by practice, and yes, by a little trial and error!

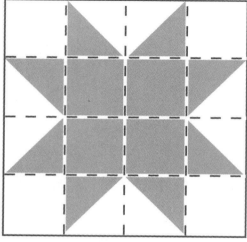

Sawtooth Star
4 x 4 Grid

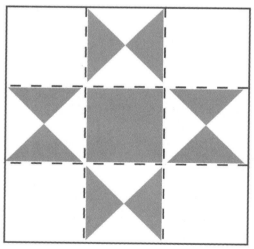

Ohio Star
3 x 3 Grid

1

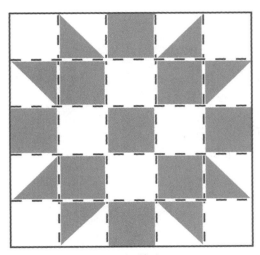

Sister's Choice
5 x 5 Grid

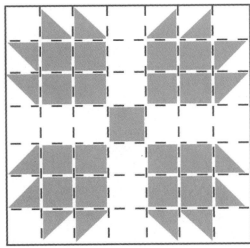

Bear's Paw
7 x 7 Grid

Once you figure out the secret patch code (a.k.a. the grid), set the Snap to Grid points at any multiple of that number. For example, if the block is based on a 4 x 4 grid, the Snap to Grid points can be set at 4 x 4, 16 x 16, or 24 x 24, etc. Because the number 24 is divisible by so many numbers, it can be used for many of the blocks we want to draw. You don't need to change it to a lower number if the grid points you need divide into it evenly. By the way, 24 x 24 is also the default Snap to Grid setting in EQ5!

Some blocks are easy to divide into a virtual grid. Others take more guesswork. Let's look at a few blocks from EQ5's Block Libraries and see how we can crack the code.

Refer to the Sawtooth Star block on the opposite page. See how the block can be divided equally into a grid of 4 x 4 squares? There are many variations of this favorite block and the majority of them can be drawn with the snap points set at 24 x 24. When you are trying to figure out the snap points for a new block, *look for a similar block* you already know.

The Ohio Star is another familiar block. Its secret patch code is 3 x 3, so it can also be drawn on a 24 x 24 grid. It's also a nine patch block, but you don't base the snap points on the number of units. Sometimes the *unit classification* (i.e. four patch, nine patch, etc.) can confuse you, so be sure to take a closer look, before basing your snap points on that alone.

Here's a five patch block, Sister's Choice, which can be drawn on a 5 x 5 grid. It's easy to spot since *all the units of the block follow the grid*.

A traditional Bear's Paw block is usually sewn as a 14" block. Its secret patch code is 7 x 7. If you know the size of the block, especially if you have a pattern from a book or magazine, *the size of the block* can help you figure out how to set up your snap points.

1

Square within a Square type blocks are a little trickier to figure out, but if you *imagine the larger triangles and squares as half-square triangles*, you can make a good guess. This one is based on a 4 x 4 grid.

For blocks like the traditional Log Cabin block, you can count the logs. This block needs an 8 x 8 grid. Even though they are still based on a square grid, if you *count the rows or logs* it's a quick way to figure out the snap points needed.

So remember these things when trying to crack the secret patch code of a pieced block:

- Look for a similar block you already know

- Check the unit classification (nine patch, four patch, etc.)

- See if the block units follow a square grid

- Find the popular size of the block – an important clue

- Imagine the larger triangles and squares as half-square triangles

- Count the rows for blocks like the Log Cabin

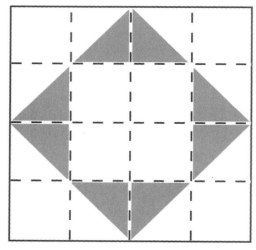

Square within a Square
4 x 4 Grid

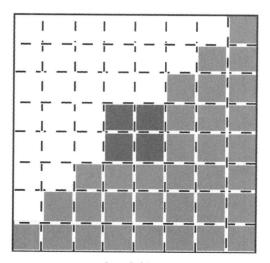

Log Cabin
8 x 8 Grid

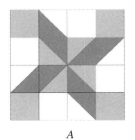

A

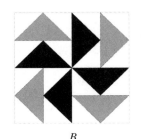

B

What's the Code?

Now it's your turn! Let's play a guessing game and see if you can figure out the secret patch code for the blocks pictured to the left. If you get stumped, the answers are at the bottom of this page. No fair peeking!

1

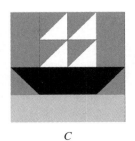

C

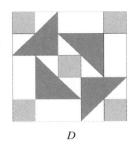

D

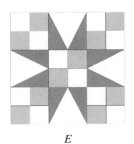

E

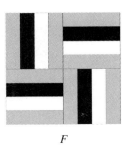

F

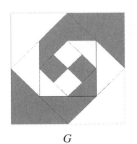

G

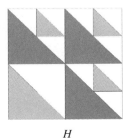

H

Drawing a New York Block

*Color block
on page 1*

Sawtooth Star Block

Between 1907 and 1912, the publication *Hearth and Home* ran a series of star blocks for each of the states in the United States. This block is a variation of the one contributed for the state of New York. We will be using the Sawtooth Star block from the previous exercise on page 12 without having to redraw it.

1 Make sure you complete the previous exercise on Drawing a Sawtooth Star block. You can open a new project file and copy the Sawtooth Star block from your User Libraries if you saved it there in the last lesson.

2 On the WORKTABLE menu, click Work on Block.

3 Click on the View Sketchbook button and select the Sawtooth Star block.

4 Click on the Edit button to place the block on the drawing board.

5 Click on the BLOCK menu again, click Drawing Board Setup.

6 On the General tab, in Snap to Grid Points, type 24 in both the Horizontal and Vertical division boxes.

7 Also on the General tab, in BlockSize, type 6 in both the Horizontal and Vertical boxes.

8 On the Graph Paper tab, in Number of Divisions, type 6 in both the Horizontal and Vertical boxes.

9 Also on the Graph Paper tab, in Options, click the down arrow on the Style box and select Graph paper lines.

10 Click OK. The graph paper lines will be visible on the drawing board now.

11 Click on the Select tool.

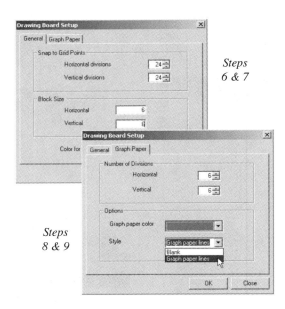

*Steps
6 & 7*

*Steps
8 & 9*

*Step 11
Select Tool*

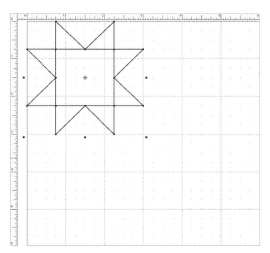

Step 16

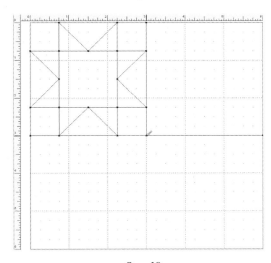

Step 19

*Step 22
Save in
Sketchbook*

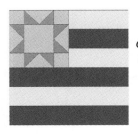

*Completed
New York
Block*

12 On the EDIT menu, click on Select All (or use the keyboard shortcut CTRL+A). The entire block will be selected.

13 While all the block lines are selected, right-click on the block to bring up the context menu and click on Resize.

14 In the Resize window, type 50 in both the Horizontal and Vertical percentage boxes.

15 Click OK. The block is now resized 50% and will fit in one quadrant of the block.

16 While the resized star block is still selected, move it up into the upper-left quadrant of the block. Take care when parking the resized block, making sure that it snaps into place.

17 Click on the Line tool.

18 Draw a horizontal line across the center of the block at 3.00".

19 Draw a vertical line at 3.00" from the top of the block to the center of the block.

20 Following the graph paper lines and spacing them 1.00" apart, draw two horizontal lines from the vertical center to the right edge of the block.

21 To complete the block, draw two more horizontal lines spacing them 1.00" apart across the bottom half of the block.

22 Click on the Save in Sketchbook button to save your block.

Drawing a Simple Paper Piecing Block

Color block on page 2

A simple paper piecing block is one that is made up of only straight lines and 45 degree angles. Simple paper piecing blocks can have more than one section or unit, but they have no odd angles to draw or to sew. As you draw your paper piecing block, EQ5 is working in the background taking out much of the guesswork.

The secret to drawing a paper piecing block is to think backwards from the way you would stitch it together. When you sew a paper piecing block, you begin with the smaller patches and work your way out to the larger ones. When you draw a paper piecing block in EQ5, you begin by drawing the larger units and then subdividing them into smaller sections or patches. Let's try drawing this little paper-pieced house, then I think you will get the picture...or should I say you will get the pattern!

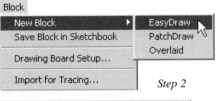

Step 2

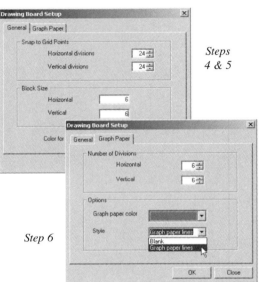

Steps 4 & 5

1 On the WORKTABLE menu, click Work on Block.

2 On the BLOCK menu, point to New Block, click EasyDraw™.

3 Click on the BLOCK menu again, click Drawing Board Setup.

4 On the General tab, in Snap to Grid points, type 24 in both the Horizontal and Vertical division boxes.

5 Also on the General tab, in Block Size, type 6 in both Horizontal and Vertical boxes.

6 On the Graph Paper tab, in Number of Divisions, type 6 in both the Horizontal and Vertical boxes. Under Options, make sure that Graph paper lines is selected in the box beside style. Click OK.

Step 6

Step 7
Line Tool

7 Click on the Line tool.

8 Draw two horizontal lines across the block – one at 2.0" and one at 5.0" from the top.

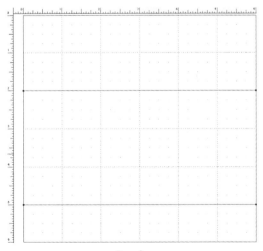

Step 8

1

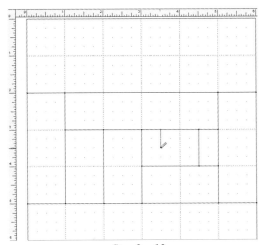

Step 9 – 13

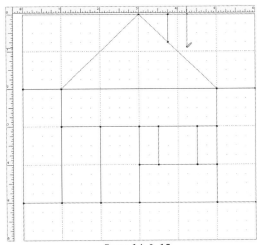

Steps 14 & 15

*Step 16
Save in Sketchbook*

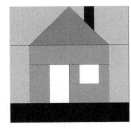

*Completed Simple
Paper Piecing Block*

Those two lines create the largest sections of this house block. This doesn't mean you will have to piece each of the larger sections as a separate unit, but they need to be drawn that way.

9 In the center section only, draw two vertical lines, one at 1.0" and one at 5.0", to create the sides of the house.

10 Draw a horizontal line between the sides of the house at 3.0". This will be the top of the door line.

11 Draw two vertical lines for the door sides, at 2.0" and at 3.0" from the top of the door line, ending at the bottom of the house.

12 Draw a horizontal line from the right side of the door to the right side of the house at 4.0" for the bottom of the window.

13 Next, draw two vertical lines between the top of the door line and the bottom of the window line at 3.5" and at 4.5".

The center section of the house is complete. Did you notice how we worked from the larger to the smaller patches?

14 To make the roof, draw two diagonal lines from the top center of the block at 3.0" to the sides of the house.

15 For the chimney, draw two vertical lines between the top of the block to the roof line, at 3.75" and at 4.25".

16 Click on the Save in Sketchbook button.

Your block is finished! Now you can check out the Print Foundation Pattern dialog box and take a look at the Print Preview. Notice how EQ5 magically calculates how to piece the block in just two units. See how the numbers for the piecing order go backwards from the way we drew the block? Keep this backwards process in mind whenever you want to create a paper piecing pattern!

Drawing a Delectable Mountains Block

Color block on page 2

1

Did you know that blocks don't have to be drawn as square blocks? A good example of a popular rectangular block is Delectable Mountains. This makes a really nice border block too!

This block doesn't seem to follow a grid. Ah...but there is a secret. Work through the exercise and then I will reveal it to you!

Delectable Mountains Block
and the Spacer Block needed for the quilt setting

1   On the WORKTABLE menu, click Work on Block.

2   On the BLOCK menu, point to New Block, click EasyDraw™.

3   Click on the BLOCK menu again, click Drawing Board Setup.

4   On the General tab, in Snap to Grid Points, type 8 in the box for Horizontal divisions and 5 for Vertical divisions.

5   Also on the General tab, in Block Size, type 8 in the box for Horizontal and 5 for Vertical.

6   On the Graph Paper tab, in Number of Divisions, type 8 in the box for Horizontal and 5 for Vertical.

7   Also on the Graph Paper tab, in Options, click the down arrow on the Style box and select Graph paper lines.

8   Click OK. The graph paper lines will be visible on the drawing board now.

9   Click on the Line tool.

10 Drawing from right to left, draw two diagonal lines. One line begins at 3.00" from the left at the top of the block and ends at 3.00" from the top on the left side. The other line begins at 5.00" from the left at the top of the block and ends at the lower-left corner.

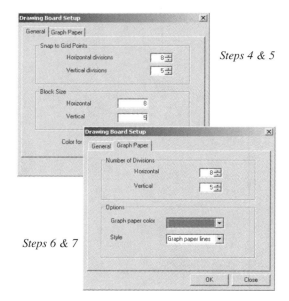

Steps 4 & 5

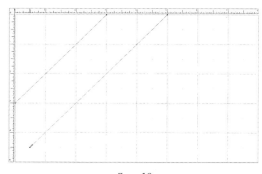

Steps 6 & 7

Step 10

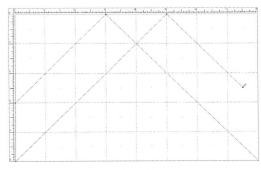

Step 11

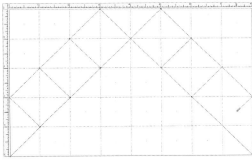

Step 12

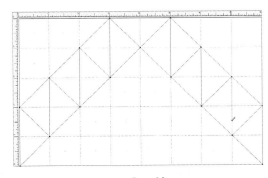

Step 13

11 Drawing from left to right, draw two diagonal lines that mirror the first two lines. One line begins at 3.00" from the left and ends at the bottom-right corner. The other line begins at 5.00" from the left and ends at 3.00" from the top on the right side of the block outline.

12 On both sides of the mountain, draw three diagonal lines spaced evenly between the diagonal lines of the mountain slopes to create three on-point squares. Let the graph paper lines guide you. These diagonal lines will fall in the square grid of the graph paper.

13 Complete the block by drawing three vertical lines in the on-point squares to create the peaks on both sides of the mountain.

14 Click on the Save in Sketchbook button to save your block.

To set your Delectable Mountains in the traditional setting, you will need a small spacer block to add between some of the blocks.

15 On the BLOCK menu, point to New Block, click EasyDraw™.

16 Click on the BLOCK menu again, click Drawing Board Setup.

1

1

17 On the General tab, in Snap to Grid Points, type 4 (you can't go lower than 4) in the box for Horizontal divisions and 5 for Vertical divisions.

18 Also on the General tab, in Block Size, type 2 in the box for Horizontal and 5 for Vertical.

19 On the Graph Paper tab, in Number of Divisions, type 2 in the box for Horizontal and 5 for Vertical.

20 Click OK.

21 Click on the Line tool.

22 Draw a diagonal line beginning at the lower-left corner and parking it at 3.00" from the top on the right side of the block.

23 Draw a second diagonal line beginning at the lower-right corner and parking it in the center at 4.00" from the top, ending at the previous line.

24 Click on the Save in Sketchbook button to save your block.

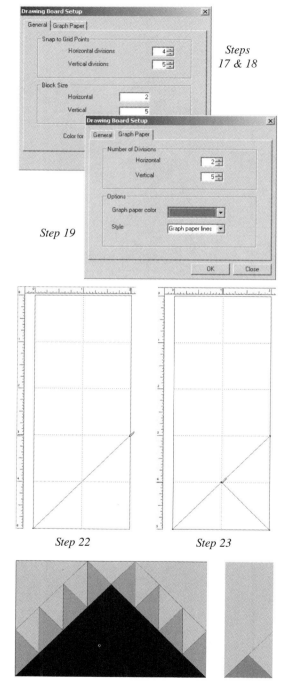

Steps 17 & 18

Step 19

Step 22   *Step 23*

Completed Delectable Mountains Block and Spacer Block

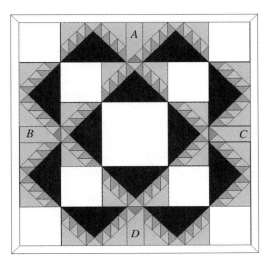

Traditional Setting for Delectable Mountains
Notice the Spacer Blocks – A,B,C & D

Try these two variations of the
Delectable Mountains Block.

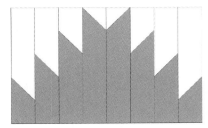

Variation 1

Variation 2

1

Tip

- To make the traditional Delectable Mountains quilt setting, you will need to use the Custom Set quilt layout. Four blocks are set around a center square (8.00"), with corner blocks added (5.00"). Each subsequent round will need to have the spacer block added between the main blocks to keep the quilt center square. The center block can be left blank to show off your quilting stitches or you can add an appliqué design.

- You can change the size of this particular Delectable Mountains block to suit your purposes, but remember to keep the size proportional: 8 to 5.

- You can also use these Delectable Mountain blocks in a border or use them in a Horizontal Strip layout. Remember to size the borders or strips proportionally (8 to 5) so that your block won't be distorted.

If you would like to try drawing one of your own blocks with fewer or more mountain peaks, you need to know the Secret Patch Code for this Delectable Mountains block, right? The secret is in the peaks!

First, decide on the number of peaks you want for your block. The horizontal snap points will be the same as the number of peaks. For the vertical snap points, divide the number of horizontal peaks by 2 and then add 1.

Number of peaks = Horizontal snap points

(Number of peaks ÷ 2) + 1 = Vertical snap points

Other things to remember when designing your own Delectable Mountains block:

* Set your block size and graph paper divisions to match the grid points or a multiple of the grid points.

* The number of peaks is always an even number. The space between the two top peaks is equivalent to 2.00".

* The width of the spacer block is always 2.00" (or equivalent to 2.00") by the height of your block.

Drawing a Block for Border & Setting Triangles

Color block on page 2

1

Let's take a different approach to drawing the Delectable Mountains block and create a block suitable for the setting triangles of an on-point quilt layout, triangles in borders, or triangles in vertical and horizontal strip layouts.

When you set blocks in the aforementioned triangles, you are actually setting an entire square block. You must rotate the block for the mountain peaks to show. To make a Delectable Mountains block for these triangles, you have to draw it as square block with the mountain peaks on one side of the center diagonal.

1   On the WORKTABLE menu, click Work on Block.

2   On the BLOCK menu, point to New Block, click EasyDraw™.

3   Click on the BLOCK menu again, click Drawing Board Setup.

4   On the General tab, in Snap to Grid Points, type 20 in both the Horizontal and Vertical division boxes.

5   Also on the General tab, in Block Size, type 5 in both the Horizontal and Vertical boxes.

6   On the Graph Paper tab, in Number of Divisions, type 5 in both the Horizontal and Vertical boxes.

7   Also on the Graph Paper tab, in Options, click the down arrow on the Style box and select Graph paper lines.

8   Click OK. The graph paper lines will be visible on the drawing board now.

9   Click on the Line tool.

10 Draw a diagonal line from the upper-right corner to the lower-left corner.

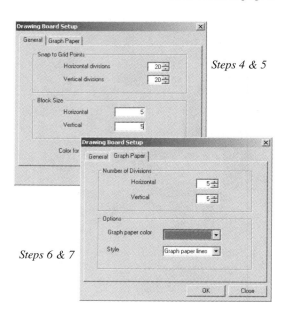

Steps 4 & 5

Steps 6 & 7

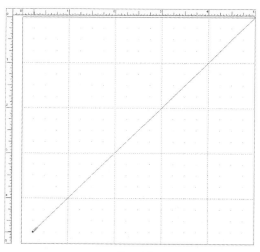

Step 10

1

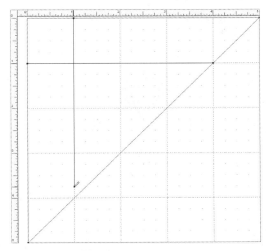

Step 12

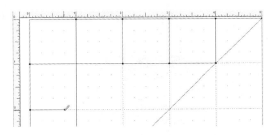

Step 13

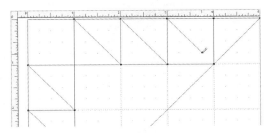

Step 14

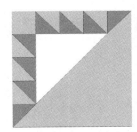

*Completed Border
& Setting Triangles*

11 Draw a horizontal line 1.00" from the top, beginning at the left side of the block and ending at the diagonal line.

12 Draw a vertical line 1.00" from the left side of the block, beginning at the top of the block and ending at the diagonal line.

13 Following the graph paper lines, draw three vertical lines 1.00" apart between the top edge of the block and horizontal line. Do the same, drawing horizontal lines 1.00" apart between the left edge of the block and the vertical line. This creates the grid to make the mountain peaks.

14 Draw three diagonal lines from left to right in each grid square on the top and left side of the block for the mountain peaks. Leave the square in the upper-left corner empty.

15 Click on the Save in Sketchbook button to save your new block.

Tip

- When you create the Delectable Mountains block in this manner, the spacer triangles are included in the block. And because it's set on the diagonal, it has a point at the top – it *is* a triangle after all!

- The secret patch code is based on the number of peaks you want on one side of your mountain. Add 2 to that number to get the snap to grid points. For example, if you want 3 peaks, set the snap points to any multiple of 5.

The Secret Patch Code of the LeMoyne Star

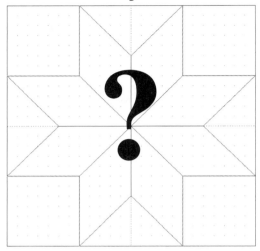

This eight-point star block goes by many names, but most quilters know it as the LeMoyne Star. Learning to draw the LeMoyne Star is an important skill to add to your EQ5 drawing capabilities since countless blocks are based on this star design. Because of the LeMoyne Star's popularity, and it's many wonderful variations, you will see it several times in this book. I highly recommend you read through this section before trying any of the variations presented in this book.

The LeMoyne Star is in a category of quilt blocks based on the division of a circle into eight equal slices. Each "slice" has an angle of 45 degrees. When we draw this basic eight-point star block in EasyDraw™, we don't need to slice up a circle. We can draw it on a grid instead. Think of it as drawing the block with just a ruler and graph paper, rather than with a compass and protractor!

I should mention that drawing the LeMoyne Star on a grid results in an eight-point star that is "almost perfect." Remember, we're drawing a circular based star on a flat grid (a round peg in a square hole?), so there is bound to be a tiny bit of size difference. This does not affect the usability of the block design or templates. Once you know the secret, you will learn how to round up patch sizes so you can rotary cut them easily. What is really cool is that EQ5 does that for us too!

Step 2

Now let's take a closer look at this special eight-point star block from the Block Library and learn about its unique secret patch code.

1   On the WORKTABLE menu, click Work on Block.

2   On the LIBRARIES menu, click on Block Library.

3   In the Block Libraries box, click on EQ Libraries to reveal the contents.

Steps 3 - 6

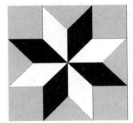

Diamond Block

4   Click on Classic Pieced.

5   Click on Eight-Point Stars. The Eight-Point Stars will appear.

6   Click on the Eight-Point Star named Diamond.

7   Click Copy to copy the block to your sketchbook.

8   Click Close to return to the Worktable.

9   Click on the View Sketchbook button.

10   In the Sketchbook, click on the Blocks tab.

11   On the Blocks tab, select the Diamond block.

12   Click on the Edit button. This will place the Diamond block on the drawing board.

13   On the BLOCK menu, click Drawing Board Setup.

Notice on the General tab, under Snap to Grid points, the Horizontal and Vertical divisions are both set at 24. EQ5 remembers the Snap to Grid points used to draw a block. It does not however, remember the block size. For this exercise we want to learn the secret patch code for drawing this block so we need to change the block size to make it easier to figure out.

Tip
- **Did you know that you can see the current Snap to Grid Points when you are on the block worktable? Look at the status bar at the bottom of the block worktable screen where it says Snap and you will see the horizontal and vertical snap points for the block. If the Status Bar is not showing, go to the VIEW menu and click to check Status bar.**

1

1

14 On the General tab, in Block Size, type 24 in both the Horizontal and Vertical boxes.

15 Click on the Graph Paper tab. Having the graph paper lines showing is optional for this exercise. But to make it easy to locate the center of the block, in Number of Divisions, type 2 for both Horizontal and Vertical.

16 Click OK to return to the drawing board. Now look at the top edge of the LeMoyne Star block again in relation to the ruler. (If the rulers are not showing on the drawing board, click on the VIEW menu and click on Rulers to check it.) Count the inches to the first star point – that's 7 inches.

17 Count the inches between the first and the second star point (the long side of triangle C) – that's 10 inches.

18 Now count the inches from the second star point to the right side of the block – that's also 7 inches.

19 Let's see, that's 7 + 10 + 7 = 24. That's it! 7 - 10 - 7 is the secret patch code for drawing the LeMoyne Star block!

Now if you are curious to know "why" this 7 - 10 - 7 works, read on...

Look at the block again. Notice that the sides of the diamond patches (A) are equal to the sides of the corner square (B) and the short sides of the triangle (C). The long side of the triangle (C) is the same length as the diagonal of the square (B). This may seem unimportant now, but you will need to know this when you are deciding what size to make the block so the patches can be rotary cut easily.

For those of you who remember their geometry lessons, this secret code is also known as the Pythagorean Theorem. Put in terms of a formula that we can use to calculate patch sizes,

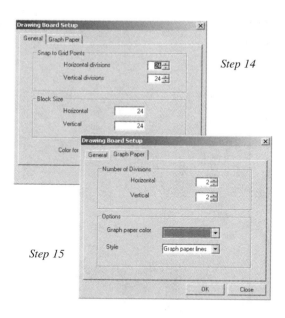

Step 14

Step 15

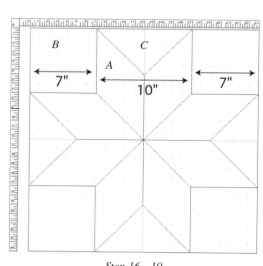

Step 16 - 19

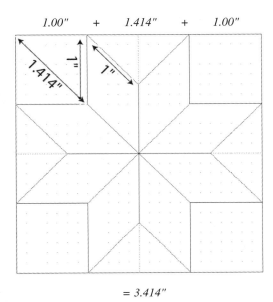

1.00" + *1.414"* + *1.00"*

= 3.414"

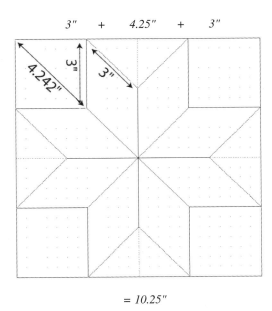

3" + *4.25"* + *3"*

= 10.25"

it means that the diagonal of a square is 1.414 times its side measurement. In other words, if sides of square B are 1.00", then the long side of triangle C would be 1.414", and total width of this block would be 3.414".

Since that's not a usable size for our grid points, we have to find a size in whole numbers instead. The closest we can come to a whole number for our grid points is to have square B equal 7.00". The diagonal of a 7.00" square is 9.898" (7 x 1.414 = 9.898, rounded up to 10.00"). That's the reason that we use 7 - 10 - 7 for the basis of our snap to grid points.

You probably don't often make a 24.00" LeMoyne Star block, right? You can use the same formula to determine what sizes are easily rotary cut and then you will know what size to print your block from EQ5. Start with the size of the square patch B. If the square is 3.00", multiply that by 1.414 to get the size of the long side of triangle C, which would be 4.242 (round that up to 4.25"). Next add the totals along the top of the block: 3.00" + 4.25" + 3.00" = 10.25".

You can also start with the finished block size. To do this, divide the finished block size by 3.414", then find the size the long side triangle C as we did before. You will know by the answer if the pieces can be easily rotary cut. Let's try a 10.00" block and see what happens. 10.00" ÷ 3.414 = 2.929" (this is the size of square B). Now let's see what the long side of triangle C would be: 2.929 x 1.414 = 4.141606. That won't work! It's definitely better to make the block 10.25".

In a later section, I'll show you how you can use this code and formula to set up the drawing board for even more eight-point star variations. I promise . . . you do not have to be a geometry whiz kid to draw these blocks! For now, just keep that secret patch code of 7-10-7 in mind, OK?

Drawing the LeMoyne Star Block

*Color block
on page 2*

Let's draw the LeMoyne Star from scratch, so you can use the skills for drawing other blocks based on this eight point star design.

1 On the WORKTABLE menu, click Work on Block.

2 On the BLOCK menu, point to New Block, click EasyDraw™. When the new block is placed on the worktable, it will have the same settings as the last block you worked on. Skip steps 3 – 8 if the settings have not been changed from the previous lesson.

3 Click on the BLOCK menu again, click Drawing Board Setup.

4 On the General tab, under Snap to Grid Points, type 24 in both the Horizontal and Vertical boxes.

5 Also on the General tab, in Block Size, type 24 in both the Horizontal and Vertical boxes.

6 On the Graph Paper tab, in Number of Divisions, type 2 in both the Horizontal and Vertical boxes.

7 Also on the Graph Paper tab, under Options, click the down arrow on the Style box and select Graph paper lines.

8 Click OK to return to the drawing board.

9 Click on the Line tool.

10 Draw two vertical lines from top to bottom, drawing one at 7.00" and one at 17.00". (Remember our secret patch code is 7 - 10 - 7.)

11 Draw two horizontal lines across the block, drawing one at 7.00" and one at 17.00".

12 On the EDIT menu, click Select All. The lines you just drew will be selected.

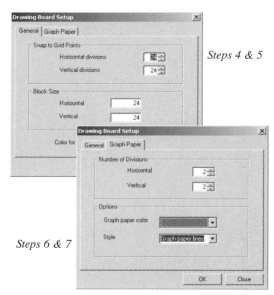

Steps 4 & 5

Steps 6 & 7

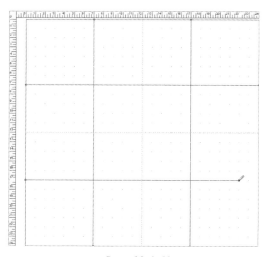

Steps 10 & 11

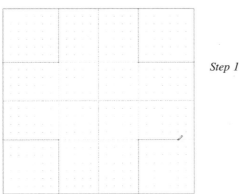

Step 14

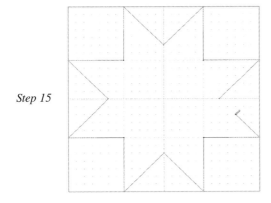

Step 15

1

13 Right-click, then click Convert to Guides. The lines will be converted to guidelines.

14 Click on the Line tool. Following the guidelines, draw the horizontal and vertical lines for all four corner squares of the LeMoyne Star.

15 Draw two 45 degree lines for the triangles between each pair of star points. Begin the diagonal line at a star point and end it in the center on the fifth grid dot from the block edge.

16 Complete the star by drawing 4 lines from opposite points in the center of the star to form the remaining diamond shapes. You will draw two diagonal lines, one horizontal line and one vertical line.

17 Click on the Save in Sketchbook button.

Try the following variations of the basic LeMoyne Star block, with a few added lines.

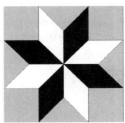

Completed Classic LeMoyne Star

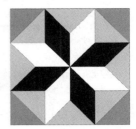

Variation 1 LeMoyne Star

Variation 2 Star of the East

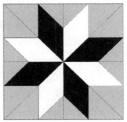

Variation 3 Paper Pieced LeMoyne Star

Step 16

Drawing a Hunter's Star Block

Color block on page 3

The Hunter's Star block is a mystery until you set it in a quilt layout. We can easily create this block using parts of a LeMoyne Star block.

1 Copy the eight-point star block called Diamond from the Block Library. (See page 32 – 33 Steps 1 – 8.)

2 Click on the View Sketchbook button.

3 In the Sketchbook, click on the Blocks tab.

4 On the Blocks tab, click to select the Diamond block.

5 Click on the Edit button. This will place the Diamond block on the worktable.

6 On the BLOCK menu, click Drawing Board Setup.

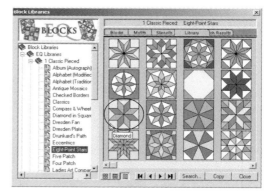

Copy the Diamond Block from the Block Library

⟍ Tip

• When you edit a block from the library, the snap points will be remembered, but not the block size. It's not necessary to change the block size to draw this block, but it will aid in drawing it. The 7-10-7 code applies to this particular block too, but this time the diamonds are against the block edge. Don't forget – graph paper lines will help you as you move the diamonds into place.

7 On the General tab, under Block Size, type 24 in both the Horizontal and Vertical division boxes.

8 On the Graph Paper tab, in Number of Divisions, type 2 in both the Horizontal and Vertical boxes. Under Options, make sure that Graph Paper lines is selected in the Style box.

9 Click OK to return to the drawing board.

10 Click on the Select tool.

11 Point the cursor just outside the block on the lower-left side and draw a selection box around the two diamonds in the lower-left quadrant.

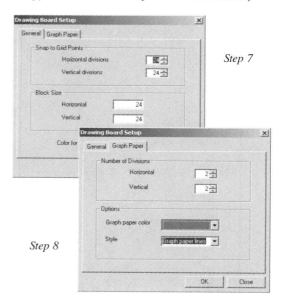

Step 7

Step 8

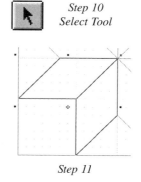

Step 10
Select Tool

Step 11

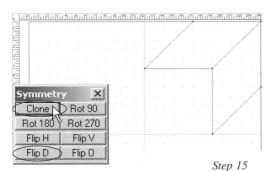

Steps 17 & 18

Step 15

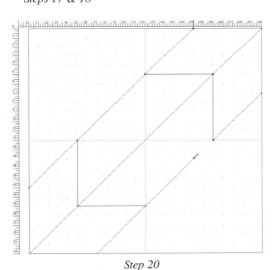

Step 20

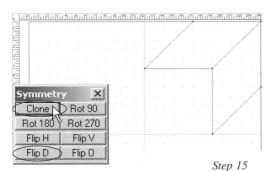

Completed Quilt

Completed Hunter's Star Block

12 With the two lower-left diamonds selected, click on the EDIT menu and click on Copy.

13 On the BLOCK menu, point to New Block, click EasyDraw™.

14 On the EDIT menu, click on Paste. The two diamonds copied from the LeMoyne Star will be placed onto your new block with a selection box around them.

15 While the diamonds are selected, drag them to the upper-right corner of the block. The two diamonds together have a right angled corner and will snap neatly into place.

16 With the diamonds still selected, click on the small black square in the corner of the Select tool to open the Symmetry box.

17 On the Symmetry box, click on Clone.

18 While the cloned pair of diamonds is still selected, click on Flip D on the Symmetry box to flip the cloned diamonds.

19 Move the selected diamonds to the lower-left corner until they snap into place.

20 Click on the Line tool. Draw three diagonal lines connecting the star points and the line in the center of the diamonds.

21 Click on the Save in Sketchbook button to save your block.

Tip

• To see the *star* of your Hunter's Star block you will need to set the blocks in a Horizontal quilt layout. Color the block as illustrated, using two contrasting colors. Set the blocks in the quilt layout, rotating them so the diamonds create an eight-point star with alternate colors where the corners of four blocks meet.

• Use the Symmetry tool to easily rotate groups of four blocks automatically. On the Quilt worktable, click on the Symmetry tool. Hold down the CTRL key, click once over the block in the upper-left corner. Voila!

Drawing a Nosegay Block

Color block on page 3

The Nosegay block is another block that can be made by editing the LeMoyne Star block.

1 Copy the eight-point star block called Diamond from the Block Library. (See page 32 – 33 Steps 1 – 8.)

2 Click on the View Sketchbook button.

3 In the Sketchbook, click on the Blocks tab.

4 On the Blocks tab, click to select the Diamond block.

5 Click on Edit. This will place the Diamond block on the worktable.

6 On the BLOCK menu, click Drawing Board Setup.

7 On the General tab, under Snap to Grid Points, type 48 in both the Horizontal and Vertical division boxes.

8 On the Graph Paper tab, under Number of Divisions, type 2 in both the Horizontal and Vertical boxes. Under Options, make sure that Graph Paper lines is selected in the Style box.

9 Click OK to return to the drawing board.

10 Click on the Select tool.

11 In the lower-right quadrant of the star block, delete the three lines forming a Y-shape around the corner square, leaving only the outside diagonal lines of the two diamonds.

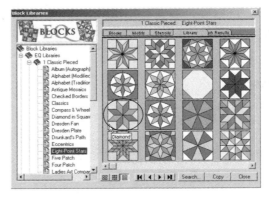

Copy the Diamond Block from the Block Library

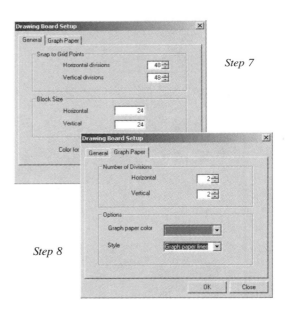

Step 7

Step 8

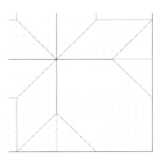

Step 11

Step 12
Edit Tool

12 Click on the Edit tool.

13 Select one of the remaining diagonal lines of the diamond and drag the node to the lower-right corner until it snaps into place. Repeat with the other diagonal line.

14 Draw the two lines that form the small squares and on-point squares between the remaining diamonds as illustrated. All lines will snap to the grid.

15 Click on the Save in Sketchbook button to save your block.

✎ Tip

- **Set the Nosegay block on-point in a quilt layout or set it in a vertical or horizontal strip quilt using the Diamonds strip style.**

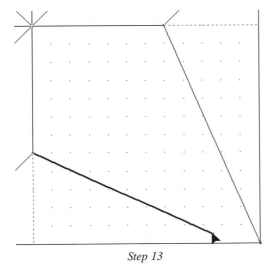

Step 13

Completed Nosegay Block

Try these variations of the Nosegay block.

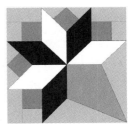

Variation 1
Draw an additional diagonal line in the kite-shaped patch to make it two parts.

Variation 2
Draw center lines in all the diamonds and in the small squares to give the nosegay a three-dimensional look.

Step 14

Drawing a Drunkard's Path Block

Color block on page 3

Learning to draw a Drunkard's Path block will teach you important drawing skills. Hundreds of blocks are based on this simple arc. This particular version is good practice for cloning and flipping.

1   On the WORKTABLE menu, click Work on Block.

2   On the BLOCK menu, point to New Block, click EasyDraw™.

3   Click on the BLOCK menu again, click Drawing Board Setup.

4   On the General tab, in Snap to Grid Points, type 24 in both the Horizontal and Vertical division boxes.

5   Also on the General tab, in Block size, type 6 in both the Horizontal and Vertical boxes.

6   On the Graph Paper tab, in Number of Divisions, type 6 in both the Horizontal and Vertical boxes.

7   Also on the Graph Paper tab, in Options, click the down arrow on the Style box and select Graph paper lines.

8   Click OK. The graph paper lines will be visible on the drawing board now.

9   Click on the Grid tool, clicking on the small black square in the lower-left corner to open the Grid Setup.

10 In Grid Setup, click the arrow buttons to change the number to 2 for both Columns and Rows.

11 Point the cursor at the upper-left corner of the block and drag the grid diagonally to the bottom-right corner and release the mouse. A 2 x 2 grid is now placed in the block.

12 Click on the Arc tool.

Drunkard's Path Block

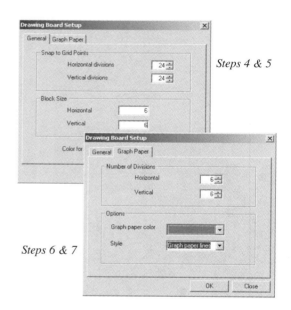

Steps 4 & 5

Steps 6 & 7

Step 10

Step 12
Arc Tool

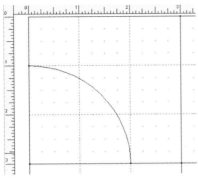

Step 13

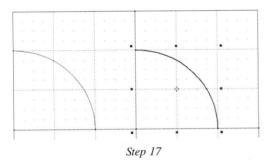

Step 17

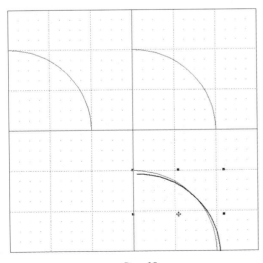

Step 19

1

✎ **Tip** ─────────────────────

- **To make an arc flip in the opposite direction, press the Spacebar on your keyboard before releasing the mouse button.**

13 In the upper-left quadrant of the block, draw an arc beginning on the left side 1.00" down from the top, and ending it on the center line at 2.00" from the left.

14 Click on the small black square on the Select tool to bring up the Symmetry box. (You can also select the arc, right-click on the drawing board and choose Symmetry from the context menu.)

15 Click on the arc you just drew, to select it.

16 On the Symmetry box, click on Clone. A new arc will appear and will automatically be selected.

17 Move the newly cloned arc to the upper-right quadrant, letting it snap into place so that it is identical to the upper-left quadrant.

18 While the second arc is still selected, click on Clone again, and move this arc to the lower right-quadrant, again making sure it snaps into place.

19 While the third arc is still selected, click on Clone again. This time the arc is not flipped in the direction we need, but we can fix that.

20 On the Symmetry box, click on Flip D. Now the arc is turned the correct way.

21 Move the arc into place in the lower-left quadrant.

22 Click on the Save in Sketchbook button to save your block.

You can color your blocks now and set them in a horizontal quilt layout. See pages 108 - 109 in the *EQ5 Design Cookbook* for directions on coloring blocks. Use the Rotate tool and Flip tool on the Quilt Worktable to arrange the blocks to create the traditional Drunkard's Path layout.

Tip

• **Try using the Symmetry tool on the Quilt Worktable to rotate the blocks. You may discover a new arrangement you like even better! As you click through the sixteen symmetry rotations, the traditional layout will eventually appear.**

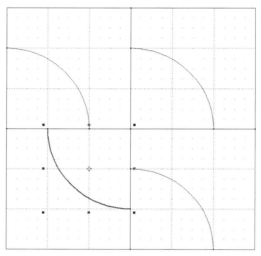

Step 21

Try these variations of the Drunkard's Path block.

Completed Drunkard's Path Block

Drunkard's Path Block Quilt

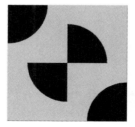

Variation 1 Drunkard's Path Block

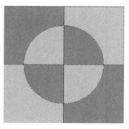

Variation 2 Drunkard's Path Block

Drawing a 1930's Posy Block

*Color block
on page 3*

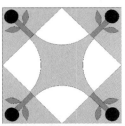

1930's Posy Block

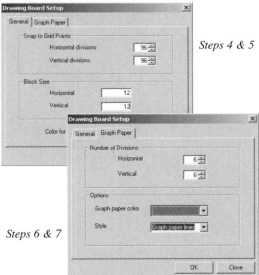

Steps 4 & 5

Steps 6 & 7

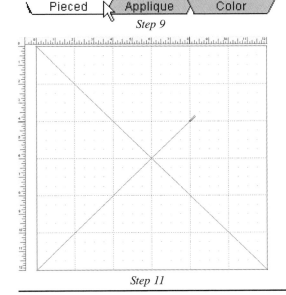

Step 9

Step 11

This variation of the 1930's Posy block is best drawn using an Overlaid block. The Overlaid style lets you use both EasyDraw™ and PatchDraw in one block. We can draw the Drunkard's Path-like part on the pieced layer and the posies on the appliqué layer.

1   On the WORKTABLE menu, click Work on Block.

2   On the BLOCK menu, point to New Block, click Overlaid.

3   Click on the BLOCK menu again, click Drawing Board Setup.

4   On the General tab, in Snap to Grid Points, type 96 in both the Horizontal and Vertical division boxes.

5   Also on the General tab, in Block Size, type 12 in both the Horizontal and Vertical boxes.

6   On the Graph Paper tab, in Number of Divisions, type 6 in both the Horizontal and Vertical boxes.

7   Also on the Graph Paper tab, in Options, click the down arrow on the Style box and select Graph paper lines.

8   Click OK. The graph paper lines will be visible on the drawing board.

9   Click on the Pieced tab at the bottom of the worktable.

10   Click on the Line tool.

11   Draw two diagonal lines from corner to corner dividing the block into four equal triangles.

12   Click on the Select tool.

1

13 Right-click on the drawing board to bring up the context menu and click Convert to Guides. The two diagonal lines will be converted to dashed lines to give you a drawing guideline.

✎ **Tip** ───────────────────

• **You can change the color of the guides in Drawing Board Setup on the General tab.**

14 Click on the Line tool.

15 Draw a square on-point inside the block outline, beginning and ending at the center points.

16 Click on the Arc tool.

17 Draw four arcs – one in each corner of the on-point square. Begin and end each arc one grid point away where the center diagonal guideline intersects with the on-point square. This is a little tricky, since you can't see the grid point, but it is there. There is a grid point exactly on the intersection of the guideline and on-point square. The next grid point over along the on-point square is where you want to park your arc. If you don't get it the first trying, use Undo (CTRL+Z) and try again.

18 Save to Sketchbook.

✎ **Tip** ───────────────────

• **It's always a good idea to save your blocks in stages as you draw them. Doing this enables you to retrieve the block later if you have to exit EQ5 or if you want to make variations of the same block. It can also be a step by step record of how you drew the block.**

19 Now we will add the posies to our block. Click on the Appliqué tab.

20 Click on the Simple Shapes tool, clicking on the small triangle in the corner of the tool to open the fly-out.

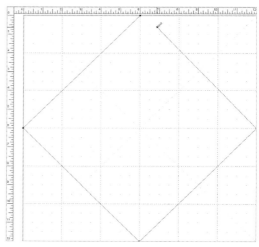

Step 15

Step 16
Arc Tool

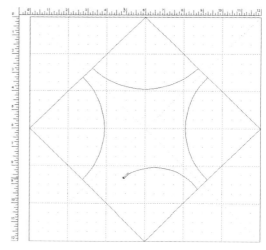

Step 17

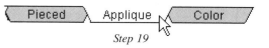

Step 19

Step 20
Simple Shapes Fly-out

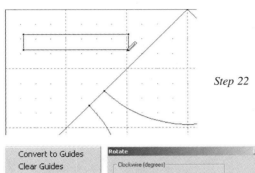

Step 22

 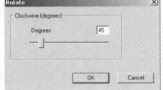

Step 25   *Step 26*

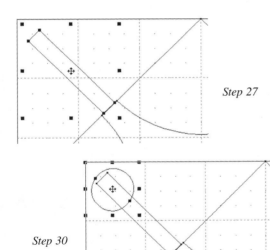

Step 27

Step 30

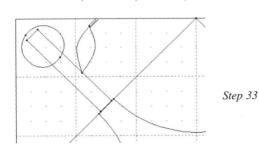

Step 33

21 On the Simple Shapes fly-out, click on the rectangle shape.

22 Point to the blank area on the upper-left corner of the block and drag the cursor diagonally from left to right to create a horizontal stem shape approximately 1/4" to 3/8" wide and 2" long – it does not have to be exact. You can adjust the size after it's drawn by clicking on the Select tool and dragging the handles as needed.

23 Click on the Select tool.

24 Click on the stem to select it.

25 With the stem selected, right-click on the drawing board and choose Rotate on the context menu.

26 In the Rotate box, type 45 for the degrees of rotation. It should be there by default unless you changed it.

27 Move the rotated stem into place where there is a gap between the arcs.

28 Click on the Simple Oval tool, clicking on the small triangle in the corner of the tool to open the fly-out.

29 Click on the circle shape.

30 Draw a circle for the posy top that's approximately 3/4" in diameter. If the circle is not centered over the stem, that's OK. Click the Select tool, click the circle and move it into place.

31 Click on the small triangle on the Simple Oval tool again to open the fly-out.

32 Click on the vertical leaf shape.

33 Point to the stem on one side and draw a leaf shape, angling it slightly upward away from the stem.

34 Click on the Select tool, clicking on the small black square to bring up the Symmetry box.

35 Click on the leaf to select it.

36 On the Symmetry box, click on Clone and then click on Flip O.

37 Move the new leaf into place on the stem opposite the first one.

38 Click anywhere away from the leaf to unselect it.

39 Point to a spot just above the top-left of the posy, hold down the left mouse button and drag the mouse diagonally. A box forms as you drag. Be sure the entire posy is enclosed before releasing the mouse. If the whole posy is not selected click away from it to deselect it, then try again.

40 On the Symmetry box, click Clone.

41 While the cloned posy is still selected, click on Rot 90.

42 While the rotated posy is still selected, move it into place in the top-right corner.

43 Repeat the Clone and Rot 90 in succession to create the remaining two posies and move them into place. Unless you have clicked off the selected patches, doing this Clone and Rot 90 goes very quickly.

44 Click on the Save in Sketchbook button to save your block.

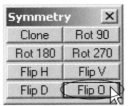

Step 36

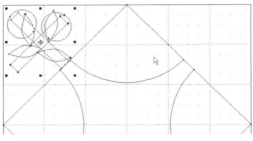

Step 41

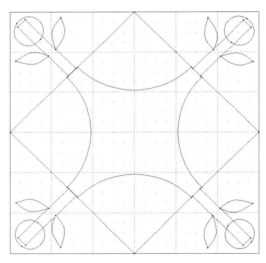

Step 43

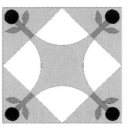

*Completed
1930's Posy
Block*

Drawing Posies in PatchDraw

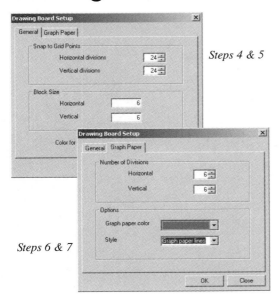

Steps 4 & 5

Steps 6 & 7

*Step 10
Polygon Tool*

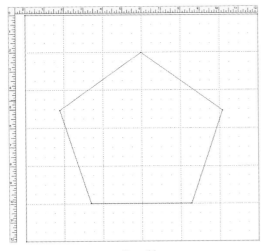

Step 11

For a quilter, a posy can be any type of simple little flower we want to appliqué onto our quilt. The number of petals is up to us. There are lots of pretty posies in the Block Libraries, but let's learn how to draw our own. In this exercise, we are going to place emphasis on making our posy parts as symmetrical as possible.

Posy Tops

1 On the WORKTABLE menu, click Work on Block.

2 On the BLOCK menu, point to New Block, click PatchDraw.

3 Click on the BLOCK menu again, click Drawing Board Setup.

4 On the General tab, in Snap to Grid Points, type 24 in both the Horizontal and Vertical division boxes.

5 Also on the General tab, in Block Size, type 6 in both the Horizontal and Vertical boxes.

6 On the Graph Paper tab, in Number of Divisions, type 6 in both the Horizontal and Vertical boxes.

7 Also on the Graph Paper tab, in Options, click the down arrow on the Style box and select Graph paper lines.

8 Click OK.

9 Click on the Polygon tool, clicking on the small triangle in the corner of the tool to open the fly-out.

10 Select the 5-sided pentagon shape.

11 Point the cursor at the drawing board about 1.00" from the top-center. (Use the graph paper lines as your guide.) While holding down the mouse button, drag downward to draw a pentagon that's about 4.00" tall.

1

12 Click on the Select tool.

13 Click on the pentagon to select it.

14 On the EDIT menu, click Copy (CTRL+C).

15 On the EDIT menu, click Paste (CTRL+V).

16 While the copied pentagon is still selected, right-click and choose Resize.

17 In the Resize box, type 44 in both the Horizontal and Vertical percentage boxes. Click OK.

18 Move the resized pentagon so that it is in the center of the larger one. The top point will be aligned with the vertical center of the block. The bottom of the pentagon will sit on the 4.00" graph line.

19 Save this block to the Sketchbook. Take a minute to name the block on the Sketchbook Notecard. Name the block "Posy Guide 5 Petals," or something similar to help you remember.

20 Click on the Select tool.

21 Click on the larger pentagon to select it. Right-click and choose Convert to Guides on the context menu.

22 Click on the Bezier Edit tool, clicking on the small black square in the corner of the tool to bring up the Edit Arc Box.

23 Click on one side of the small pentagon and then click on To Curve on the Edit Arc box. Repeat this step, so that all five sides are converted to curves.

24 Point to any handle on the small pentagon and drag it so it rests on the guideline a short distance from the point of the large pentagon.

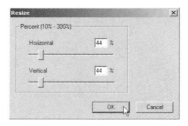

Step 17

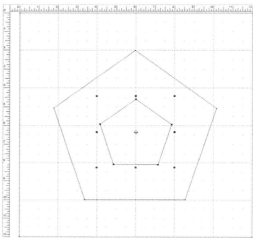

Step 18

Step 22
Bezier Edit Tool

Step 23

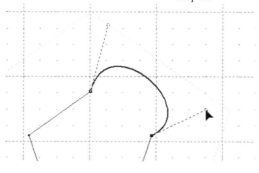

Step 24

1

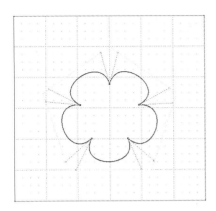

Step 25

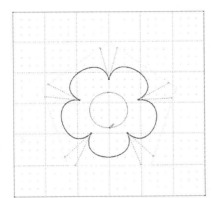

Step 29

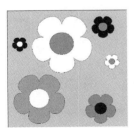

Save several sizes of your Posies Block in the User Libraries.

Step 4

Tip
- **If you hold down the SHIFT key and click on all sides of the pentagon in succession, you will be able to see all the handles at the same time.**

25 Repeat the previous step, spacing the handles an equal distance from the points of the larger pentagon. Since this is not an exact science, you will have to eyeball the distance from the points.

26 Once you are happy with the curve of the petals, click on the Save in Sketchbook button to save your block.

27 Now you can add a center to your posy. Click on the Simple Oval tool, clicking on the small triangle in the corner of the tool to open the fly-out.

28 Click on the circle shape.

29 Point the cursor at the center of the posy and drag the cursor downward to draw a circle. Once you have the circle drawn, you can use the Select tool to resize or move it if you like.

Tip
- **Group several sizes of your posies on one block and save them in the User Libraries for easy access from any project file.**

Posy Leaves
Let's try making a symmetrical leaf!

1 On the BLOCK menu, point to New Block, click PatchDraw.

2 Keep the same settings you had for drawing Posy Tops. Unless you have worked on another block, the settings will be the same. (See steps 3 - 8 under Posy Tops on page 49.)

3 Click the small triangle in the corner of the Simple Oval tool to open the fly-out.

4 Click on the vertical leaf shape.

1

5   Point the cursor at the block in the center 1.00" from the top and drag the mouse downward to draw a leaf that is 3.00" tall.

6   Click on the Bezier Edit tool.

7   Holding down the SHIFT key, click on both sides of the leaf shape so that you can see all four handles at the same time.

8   Drag each of the four handles so that they make a 45 degree angle from the leaf point in the adjacent square of the graph paper grid, placing the end of the handle at the intersection of the grid.

9   Click on the Save in Sketchbook button.

10   Now let's try some other leaf variations on the same block. First, move the leaf that's on the block out of the way. Click on the Select tool, click on the leaf to select it and move it up to the left corner of the block.

11   Click on the small triangle in the corner of the Simple Oval tool, then click on the vertical leaf shape again.

12   This time we are going to drag and draw the leaf diagonally. Point the cursor at a graph paper intersection and drag it diagonally so that the leaf is drawn at a 45 degree angle in a 2.00" square grid on the block.

13   Click on the Bezier Edit tool.

14   Holding down the SHIFT key, click on both sides of the new leaf so that you can see all four handles at the same time.

15   Drag each of the handles and place them 1.00" from the leaf points so that they make a right angle from the leaf point.

16   Click on the Save in Sketchbook button to save this leaf too. This is a narrower leaf than the one we drew vertically.

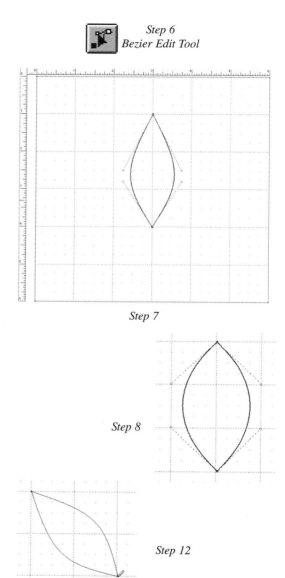

Step 6
Bezier Edit Tool

Step 7

Step 8

Step 12

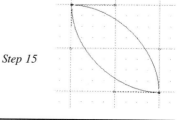

Step 15

1

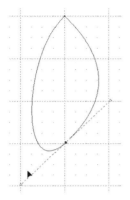

Step 25

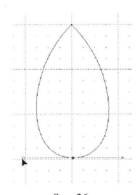

Step 26

You can make one leaf in several different sizes by using Resize on the right-click context menu.

17 Click on the Select tool.

18 Click on your new leaf and move it out of the way on the block. Let's try one more leaf.

19 Click on the first leaf to select it.

20 On the EDIT menu, click Copy (CTRL+C).

21 On the EDIT menu, click Paste (CTRL+V).

22 Move the copied leaf to an empty space on the block, centering the leaf on a vertical graph paper line.

23 Click on the Bezier Edit tool, clicking on the small black square to bring up the Edit Node box.

24 Click on the bottom node of the leaf.

25 On the Edit Node box, click on Symm. Notice that the bottom of the leaf now has a curve instead of a point. When you click on Symm on the Edit Node box, you can drag one handle and the opposite one will drag simultaneously. This keeps the line on either side of the node symmetrical.

26 Drag one of the handles until they are horizontal to the node, making the bottom of the leaf nice and round.

27 Click on Save in Sketchbook.

Tip

- I like to create several leaves on one block and then I save them in the User Libraries (pages 14 – 17) so that I can use them in other projects. You can create several different leaves on one block or you can create one leaf in different sizes. To make different sizes without distorting the leaf, use Resize on the right-click context menu to make several sizes of one leaf.

- In addition to saving your leaves as a block, you might also want to delete the block outline and save them as motifs.

Tracing Letters in PatchDraw

Color block on page 4

Did you ever want to create appliqué lettering to use on your quilts? The tracing feature in EQ5 makes it easy! In this exercise we will use Microsoft Paint™ to type the letters and save them as a bitmap. Then we can import them into EQ5 for tracing.

Appliqué Letters

1   On the Windows desktop, click on the Start menu, point to Programs, point to Accessories and click on Paint™.

2   In Microsoft Paint™, the white background may or may not be sized for our purpose. To change this, click the IMAGE menu, click on Attributes.

3   In Attributes, type 450 in both the Width and Height boxes.

4   Under Units, click to check pixels.

5   Under Colors, click to check colors.

6   Click OK. This will change the size of the white background so that we have room to type our practice letters.

7   Click on the Text tool. It looks like the letter A with a box around it.

8   Point the cursor (which has changed to a crosshair) on the left side about halfway down on the white workspace and click. A text box will appear and the cursor will be flashing, ready for typing text.

9   Before typing any letters, you need to change the text size and font. You must have a text box showing on the workspace before you can do this next step. Click on the VIEW menu.

10 On the VIEW menu, click to check Text toolbar. The Text toolbar will appear. It's a floating toolbar, so you can move it to a different place if needed.

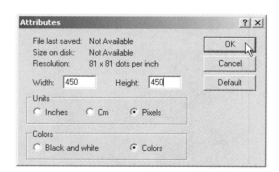

Step 1

Steps 3 - 5

Step 7
Text Tool

Steps 11-13
As seen in most versions of Windows

Steps 11 - 13
As seen in Windows XP

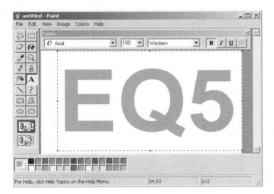

Step 15

Steps 18 - 20

11 On the Text Toolbar, click the down arrow beside the box showing the font names and select Arial Western. (In Windows XP, Western is in a separate drop down list).

12 In the size box, highlight the number that is currently there and type 150 (the drop down list only goes up to 72, so this is a workaround to get a larger size). Press the Enter key on your keyboard after typing the number.

13 Also on the Text toolbar, click on the B to make the font Bold.

14 Click inside the text box, or point the cursor at the far left of the white workspace and click to form a new text box.

15 Type in the text: EQ5. These letters and the number 5 contain all the elements you will need to learn for tracing letters.

16 While the cursor is still blinking in the text box, click on the red color on the Color Box at the bottom of the window. The text will change to red and make it much easier to see for tracing. If you click off the text box, you can use the Fill tool in Paint to color the letters red. (Note: if the Color Box is not showing, click on the VIEW menu and click to check Color Box.

17 On the FILE menu, click Save As.

18 In Save As, click the down arrow beside the Save In box and navigate to a folder where you would like to save your letters image and select it. (Suggestion: C:\My Documents\My EQ5\BMP)

19 Also in the Save As box, type a name of your choice in the File name box.

20 Click the down arrow beside the Save As type box and select 24-bit Bitmap.

1

21 Click Save.

22 In EQ5, on the WORKTABLE menu, click Work on Block.

23 On the BLOCK menu, point to New Block, click PatchDraw.

24 Click on the BLOCK menu again, click Drawing Board Setup.

25 On the General tab, in Snap to Grid Points, type 24 in both the Horizontal and Vertical division boxes.

26 Also on the General tab, in Block Size, type 6 in both the Horizontal and Vertical boxes.

27 On the Graph Paper tab, in Number of Divisions, type 4 in both the Horizontal and Vertical boxes. Under Options, make sure that Graph paper lines is selected. Click OK.

28 On the BLOCK menu, click Import for Tracing.

29 In Import for Tracing, navigate to the folder where you saved your letters image and select the file so that the name appears in the File name box.

30 Click Open. The bitmap will be placed on the drawing board and a Bitmap tab will appear at the bottom of the worktable along with the PatchDraw and Color tabs. When a bitmap is imported for tracing, you are automatically on the Bitmap tab.

✎ Tip

• **When a bitmap is imported for tracing in EQ5, it is placed in the upper-left corner of the drawing board. It may or may not fit within the block outline. Sometimes this is OK, but if it's not, you can resize the bitmap, move it around and even crop it to make it fit the worktable the way you like. See pages 160 - 161 of the *EQ5 Design Cookbook* for instructions.**

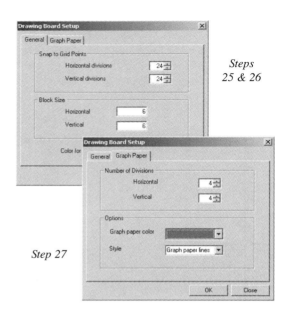

Steps 25 & 26

Step 27

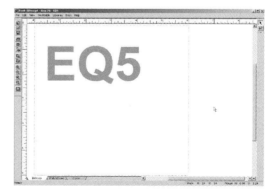

Step 28

Step 30

1

Step 31

Step 32

Step 33
Zoom Tool

Step 34
Line Tool

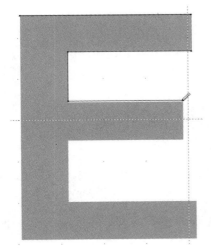

Step 35

31 On the Bitmap tab, point the cursor at the letters image bitmap and click once. The outline of the bitmap will appear. The bitmap outline has black handles on the corners and sides. The PatchDraw block outline is just a dotted line without handles. You can move the bitmap around by clicking on it and holding down the left mouse button. It is likely you will not need to resize or crop the bitmap, since the lettering should fit well within the block outline. Once the letters are traced, resize them as desired.

32 Click on the PatchDraw tab.

33 Trace the letters in order, beginning with the E. First, let's zoom in on our letter to make it easier to see for tracing. Click on the Zoom tool. Point the cursor near the E and draw a box around it while holding down the left mouse button. The viewing screen will zoom in on the area where you draw the box.

34 Click on the Line tool.

35 Begin tracing the E on the upper left corner. As you trace the letters, always draw in one direction, clockwise or counterclockwise. This makes it much easier to get a closed patch. Release the mouse quickly when you come to a corner and need to change direction. Don't worry if this initial tracing looks messy, you can fine tune your drawing once you are sure you have a closed patch.

Tip

• When you are tracing around the bitmap and need to change direction or add a node for a curve, do it with a quick, "release, click and hold" of the left mouse button. Don't move the mouse away from the node when you release it. EQ5 has an Auto-join feature that joins the nodes if within range. If you move the mouse away, you may leave a gap in your patch.

1

36 Once you have traced around the E, you can check to see if it is closed patch. Click on the Bezier Edit tool and point to any node without clicking the mouse button. The tooltip message will tell you if your patch is closed or open. If the patch is open, the steps at the end of this lesson will show you how to join the nodes.

Now let's trace the letter Q. This letter has a hollow center so we need to trace it so that the background can show through. Other letters with hollow centers and parts can be done in the same way. Choose an area on the letter where you can easily draw a channel to the hollow area. For the Q, I arbitrarily decided to make the channel near the squiggle part. Note that the patch is still traced as one piece.

37 Click on the Bezier tool.

38 Trace around the letter Q, going in one direction and ending up at the same node where you began. *Release the mouse at key turning points* to establish nodes, leaving the open channel. Leave adequate space between the squiggle and the other side so that it is easier to draw and to avoid nodes snapping together in the wrong place. *Don't worry about neatness* as you go around the first time, you can fine tune when the shape is completely traced.

39 Click on the Bezier Edit tool. Click on nodes and use the handles to adjust the shape. Close the channel gap by moving nodes and adjusting handles to make it match up with the other side. Try not to overlap the design, it will show in the finished block.

40 Let's trace the number 5. The shape has both lines and curves, no problem for EQ5!

41 Click on the Line tool.

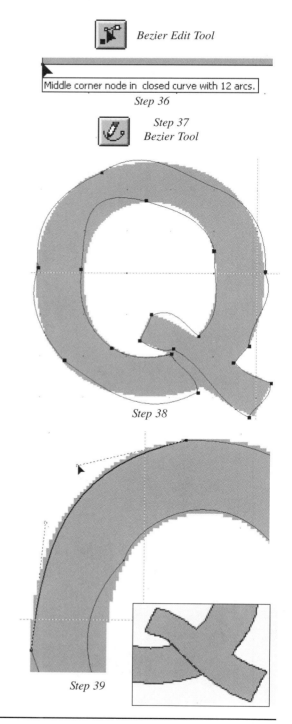

Bezier Edit Tool

Middle corner node in closed curve with 12 arcs.

Step 36

Step 37
Bezier Tool

Step 38

Step 39

1

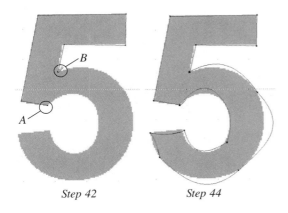

Step 42   *Step 44*

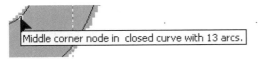

Middle corner node in closed curve with 13 arcs.

Step 45
To find an open node, look for the tooltip message:
Initial (of Final) node in an open curve.

Completed Traced Letters

Completed
Appliqué Letters placed
over the EQ Logo block

42 Going clockwise, begin tracing the 5 at point A. Continue drawing, following the outline of the 5, to point B.

43 Click on the Bezier tool.

44 Point the cursor exactly at the end node at point B. Finish tracing the curved bottom and end up at point A.

45 To see if your patch is closed, click on the Bezier Edit tool and point without clicking to any node on the patch. If the tooltip message says that the patch is open, you will need to find the open nodes and join them. If the patch is closed, skip the next paragraph and continue with the last step.

If your patch has an open curve, you first need to find the culprit. It may help to zoom in to get a closer look. Click on the Zoom tool and drag a box around the area you want to enlarge. Click on the Bezier Edit tool. When you find the open nodes, click and drag one of the nodes so it is on top of the other node. The Auto-join feature will join the nodes.

46 Click on the Bezier Edit tool. Click on nodes and use the handles to adjust the shape. Click on the Save in Sketchbook button. Click on the Color tab and color the block if you like.

Tip
- **If you want to add the letters to another block or to a quilt layer, delete the block outline and save the letters as a motif.**

Try this block with your new letters. Copy the EQ Logo block from the Block Libraries under Contemporary Pieced, Home Delights. Copy and paste the EQ Logo block onto the pieced layer on an Overlaid block. Then copy the EQ5 letters onto the Appliqué layer of the block.

Drawing a Flower Basket Block

*Color block
on page 4*

1

Flower Baskets are a combination of pieced and appliqué techniques. That's no problem for EQ5! We can use the Overlaid block style and draw both on the same block.

Flower Basket Block

1 On the WORKTABLE menu, click Work on Block.

2 On the BLOCK menu, point to New Block, click Overlaid.

3 Click on the BLOCK menu again, click Drawing Board Setup.

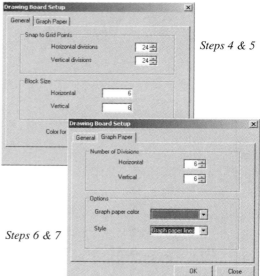

Steps 4 & 5

4 On the General tab, in Snap to Grid Points, type 24 in both the Horizontal and Vertical division boxes.

5 Also on the General tab, in Block Size, type 6 in both the Horizontal and Vertical boxes.

6 On the Graph Paper tab, in Number of Divisions, type 6 in both the Horizontal and Vertical boxes.

Steps 6 & 7

7 Also on the Graph Paper tab, in Options, click the down arrow on the Style box and select Graph paper lines.

8 Click OK. When you return to the drawing board, you should automatically be on the Pieced layer.

9 Click on the Line tool.

10 Draw a diagonal from the upper right corner to the lower-left corner.

11 Draw another diagonal line from right to left for the bottom of the basket, beginning at 4.00" from the top and ending at 4.00" from the left.

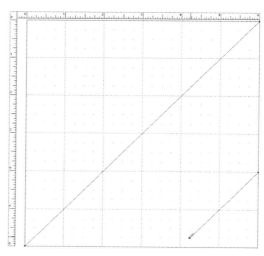

Step 11

1

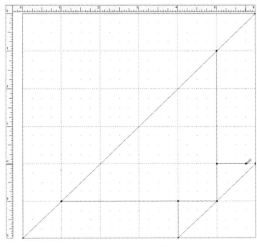

Steps 12 – 14

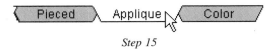

Step 15

Step 16
Bezier Tool

Step 17
Begin drawing at the 1.50" grid point

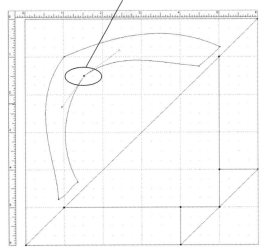

12 Draw a horizontal line for one side of the basket, beginning at 5.00" from the top on the center diagonal line and ending at 5.00" from the left.

13 Draw a vertical line for the other side of the basket, beginning 5.00" from the left on the center diagonal line and ending at 5.00" from the top.

14 Draw two 1.00" lines, one vertical and one horizontal, at the 4.00" graph paper grid intersection to the block outline to complete the bottom of the basket.

15 Click on the Appliqué tab.

16 Click on the Bezier tool.

We're going to begin drawing at the top-center of the handle. Starting at the top of the handle makes it easier to see where we began, and ensures that we will end up with a closed patch. We also want to establish nodes at the top of the handle so that we can make it symmetrical.

17 Point the cursor near the 1.50" grid point and begin drawing the handle. Draw in one direction, clockwise or counterclockwise, and end the patch at the same node where you began. Stop and release the mouse when changing direction to establish nodes for the bottom ends of the handle. There are 6 nodes total needed for the handle.

Don't worry if the bottom ends of your handle don't meet the basket yet. In fact, you will find it easier to see your complete patch if they are not. When you first draw the handle it won't look much like a handle, but that's ok, we will fine tune it after we get our closed patch.

1

⟍Tip

- **Remember that you can check to see if your patch is closed by using the Bezier Edit tool. Without clicking, point to any node on your handle. The tooltip message will magically pop up to tell you if your patch is closed or open.**

Now let's fix this thing we drew and make it look more like a basket handle!

18 Click on the Bezier Edit tool, clicking on the small black square in the corner of the tool to bring up the Edit Arc box.

19 Click on each of the short end curves of the basket handle, one at a time, to select them. On the Edit Arc box, click on To Line to make them straight lines instead of curves.

20 Move these flat ends of the basket handle to line up with the center diagonal line that makes the top of the basket. In their respective directions, the inside-corner node of the handle should rest near the 4.50" grid point 1.50" in from the block outline. The outside-corner node should rest near the 4.75" grid point.

21 Click on the center node of the inside curve at the top of the basket handle. On the Edit Node box, click on Symm. This will make the node handles move at the same time to keep the curves on either side symmetrical.

22 Drag one of the node handles to the 2.50" grid point. The handle lines will be at a 45 degree angle.

23 Click on the center node of the outside curve at the top of the basket handle. Again, on the Edit Node box, click on Symm.

24 Drag one of the node handles to the block outline at 2.50".

Step 18
Bezier Edit Tool

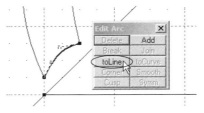

Step 19

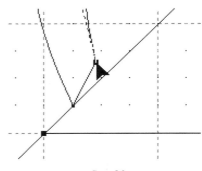

Step 20

Step 22
Drag node handle to the 2.50" grid point

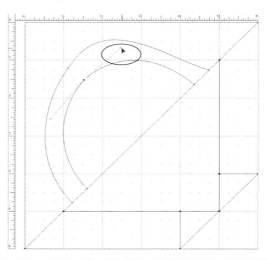

1

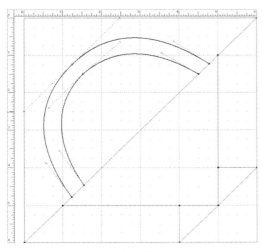

Step 25

✒ **Tip**

• **This is not an exact science, since the adjusting handles do not snap to the grid points. However, you can get pretty close if you observe the mouse position on the Status bar or watch the mouse position on the rulers, as you drag to place the handles.**

25 Click on each of the curves and adjust the bottom node handles to make the width of the basket handle as uniform as possible. To see all handles at the same time, hold down the SHIFT key and click on each curve.

26 Click on the Save in Sketchbook button to save your block.

*Completed Flower
Basket Block*

Try these variations of the Flower Basket block. For the baskets with triangles, use the graph paper lines as your guide for dividing the basket into triangles. The basket with posies is made by copying and pasting some of the posies and leaves we drew on pages 49 – 53 onto the appliqué layer of the basket block. Feel free to use your imagination to create your own unique flower basket.

*Variation 1
Flower Basket Block*

*Variation 2
Flower Basket Block*

*Variation 3
Flower Basket Block*

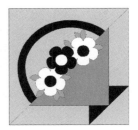

*Variation 4
Flower Basket Block*

Drawing a Tree of Life Block

*Color block
on page 4*

The Tree of Life block appears to be complicated due to its many pieces, but no advanced tools are needed, just a little EQ5 know-how! To draw this block, we will use many of the skills you have learned in this chapter. This block has many variations, but thinking ahead, I chose this one because it's easy to sew!

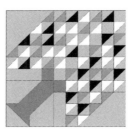

Tree of Life Block

1 On the WORKTABLE menu, click Work on Block.

2 On the BLOCK menu, point to New Block, click EasyDraw™.

3 Click on the BLOCK menu again, click Drawing Board Setup.

4 On the General tab, in Snap to Grid Points, type 20 in both the Horizontal and Vertical division boxes.

5 Also on the General tab, in Block Size, type 10 in both the Horizontal and Vertical boxes.

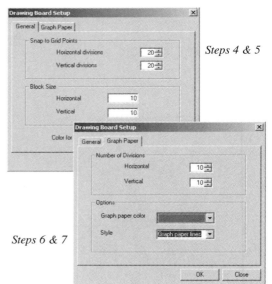

Steps 4 & 5

6 On the Graph Paper tab, in Number of Divisions, type 10 in both the Horizontal and Vertical boxes.

7 On the Graph Paper tab, in Options, click the down arrow on the Style box and select Graph paper lines. Click OK.

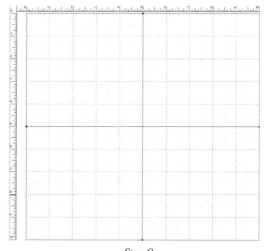

Steps 6 & 7

8 Click on the Line tool.

9 Following the graph paper lines, draw a horizontal and a vertical line in the center of the block to divide it into a four patch.

Step 9

1

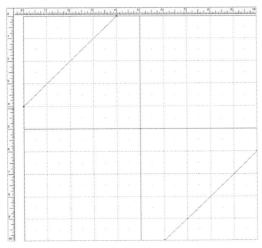

Step 10

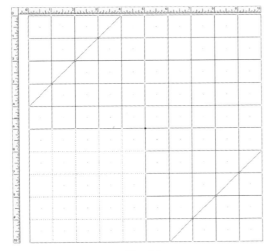

Step 13

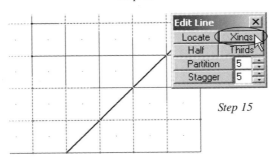

Step 15

10 Draw two diagonal lines. Draw one in the upper-left hand quadrant, beginning at 4.00" from the top and ending at 4.00" from the left. Draw the second line in the lower-right quadrant, beginning at 6.00" from the left and ending at 6.00" from the top.

11 Click on the Grid tool, clicking on the small black square in the corner to bring up the Grid Setup box.

12 In the Grid Setup box, use the arrow buttons to increase both the columns and rows to 5.

13 Use the Grid tool to create a 5 x 5 grid in the upper-left, upper-right and lower-right quadrants of the block. To do this, point the cursor at the upper-left corner of the quadrant. Holding down the left mouse button, drag the mouse diagonally to the bottom-right corner of the quadrant to create a 5 x 5 grid. Do NOT save it to the Sketchbook yet!

14 Click on the small black square of the Edit tool to bring up the Edit Line box.

15 Click on one of the diagonal lines from Step 10 to select it. On the Edit Line box, click on Xings. Repeat with the other diagonal line.

Using the Xings feature to establish nodes only along the diagonal line makes it easier to delete parts of the grid we created that will not be needed in the final block. If you save it to the Sketchbook before remembering to use Xings, you will have a lot more clicking to delete those unwanted lines!

16 Click on the Select tool.

1

17 Holding down the SHIFT key, click to select all the lines that are to the left of the diagonal line in the upper-left quadrant. Do the same for the lines to the right of the diagonal line in the lower-right quadrant. Press the DELETE key on your keyboard.

18 Now you can save the block to the Sketchbook!

19 Click on the Line tool.

20 To create the tree top, draw diagonal lines as illustrated to create small half-square triangles. Notice that there is no diagonal line drawn from the block center to the upper-right corner. These squares are to remain open.

21 To create the top of the tree trunk, draw a horizontal line in the lower-left quadrant at 6.00" from the top, and a vertical line at 4.00" from the left ending at the nodes on the tree top. This creates a square in the upper-right corner of this quadrant.

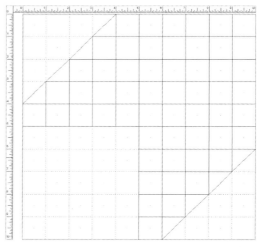

Step 17

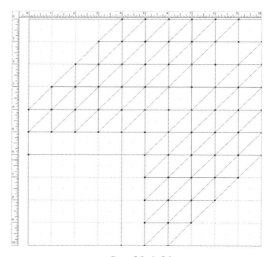

Step 20 & 21

1

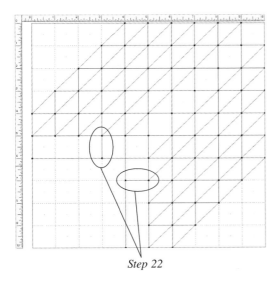

Step 22

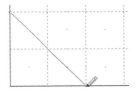

Step 24

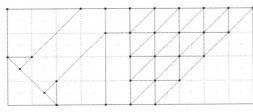

Steps 25 & 26

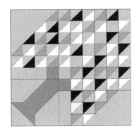

*Completed
Tree of Life Block*

22 Using the graph paper lines as your guide, draw two short lines to create a 1.00" square next to the square you just created.

23 Save the block to the Sketchbook to establish nodes.

24 Draw a diagonal line in the lower-left corner, beginning the line at 8.00" from the top and ending at 2.00" from the left on the block outline.

25 To create the tree's trunk, draw two diagonal lines going from right to left. Begin the lines at the node on the top of the tree trunk and end them at the diagonal line you created in the left corner.

26 To complete the base of the tree draw two short lines from the tree trunk to the block outline, using the graph paper lines as your guide.

27 Click on the Save in Sketchbook button to save your block and color it!

\Tip ───────────────

• This block is most often made on a larger scale and set on-point as the center in a medallion style quilt. Keep in mind the finished size of the half-square triangles when deciding how large to make the block. For instance, if the finished block size is 20.00", the half-square triangles in the tree top will be 2.00".

Chapter 2 Color Illustrations

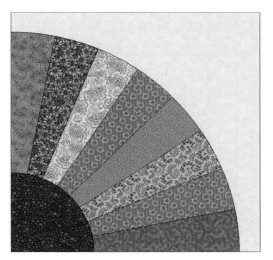

Grandmother's Fan
Page 81

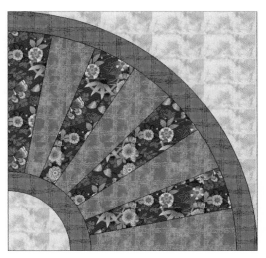

Grandmother's Fan Variation
Page 81

2

Grandmother's Fan Variation
Page 81

2

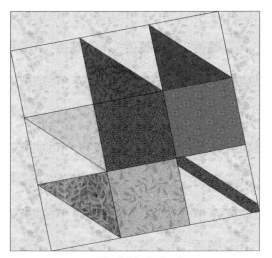

Tilted Maple Leaf
Page 83

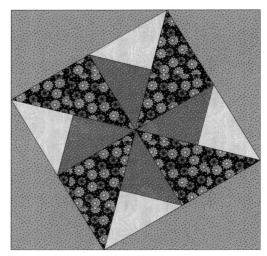

Tilted Pinwheel
Page 83

Lone Star
Page 86

Random String-Pieced
Page 88

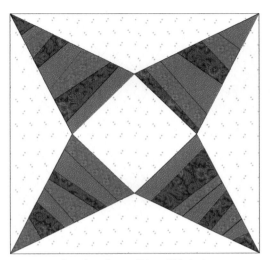

Random String-Pieced Variation
Page 88

Random String-Pieced Variation
Page 88

2

Crazy Patch Star
Page 90

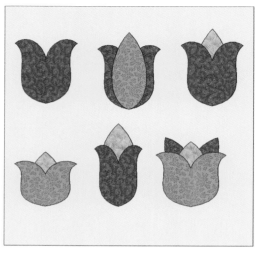

Folk Art Tulip Tops
Page 91

Folk Art Tulip Wreath
Page 96

Thin Lines & Curves as Closed Shapes
Page 113

Drawing with Advanced Drawing Features

Chapter 2

Chapter 2 Overview

In the first chapter, all the exercises were done using only the five basic drawing tools. You also learned to use the many drawing aids EQ5 has to offer. Now you are ready to use the advanced drawing features, and will learn that EQ5 has more drawing potential than you ever thought possible! This chapter is designed to familiarize you with using the advanced drawing features in EasyDraw™ and PatchDraw. Some of the blocks may look familiar to you and others will inspire you to take EQ5 to new heights in drawing!

2

Adding the Advanced Drawing Features

This section will show you how to turn on the advanced drawing features and add some of the tools to the drawing toolbar.

Adding the Features

1. On the WORKTABLE menu, click Work on Block.

2. On the FILE menu, click Preferences.

3. Click the Drawing Options tab.

4. Click the box next to *Customize the drawing toolbars* to add a check.

5. Click the box next to *Advanced drawing features* to add a check.

6. Click OK.

Customizing the EasyDraw™ Toolbar

1. On the BLOCK menu, point to New Block, click EasyDraw™.

2. Position your cursor over the EasyDraw™ tools on the right toolbar and right-click. The Customize Toolbar box will display buttons for all the drawing functions possible in EasyDraw™. Some of these tools are not on the toolbar by default. You may add as many of them to your toolbar as you like.

3. Position your cursor over the Snap to Grid tool on the Customize Toolbar box. Click, hold and drag it over to the right toolbar. Position it just under the Grid tool already there. You will see a dark line under the Grid tool when it is ok to release your mouse button.

4. Repeat the process in Step 3 to add the Snap to Node, Snap to Drawing, and Hide/Show Graph Paper tools.

5. Click the Close button to close the Customize Toolbar box.

Step 2 Adding the features

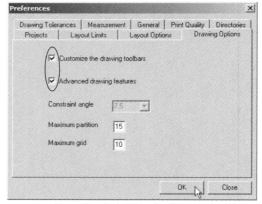

Steps 3 – 6 Adding the features

Step 2 Customizing the EasyDraw™ Toolbar

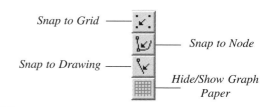

Snap to Grid

Snap to Node

Snap to Drawing

Hide/Show Graph Paper

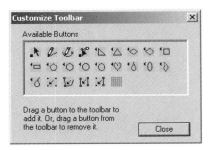

Step 3 Customizing the PatchDraw Toolbar

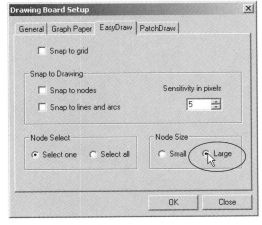

Snap to Grid ——

Auto Align Similar
Lines

Hide/Show Graph
Paper ——

—— Snap to Node

—— Snap Patch to Grid

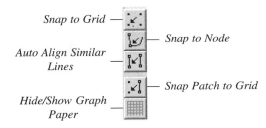

Tip: Change the node size to large

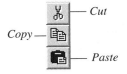

—— Cut

Copy ——

—— Paste

Customizing the PatchDraw Toolbar

1 On the BLOCK menu, point to New Block, click PatchDraw.

2 Position your cursor over the PatchDraw tools on the right toolbar and right-click. The Customize Toolbar box will display buttons for all the drawing functions possible in PatchDraw. You will see some different buttons than those in EasyDraw™.

3 Position your cursor over the Snap to Grid tool on the Customize Toolbar box. Click, hold, and drag it over to the right toolbar. Position it just under the Simple Oval tool already there. You will see a dark line under the Simple Oval tool when it is ok to release your mouse button.

4 Repeat the process in Step 3 to add the Snap to Node, Auto Align Similar Lines, Snap Patch to Grid, and Hide/Show Graph Paper tools.

5 Click the Close button.

Tip
- **You can make the nodes appear larger in EasyDraw™. Once you have turned on the Advanced Drawing Features, on the BLOCK menu, click Drawing Board Setup. In Drawing Board Setup, click on the EasyDraw™ tab. Under Node size, check the circle beside Large and then click OK.**

Adding the Edit Tools

To add the edit tools to the left toolbar, on the VIEW menu click on Edit Tools to check it. This will add the Cut, Copy and Paste tools to the left toolbar, making it much easier to cut, copy, and paste.

Overview of the Advanced Drawing Tools

This section is an overview of each of the
advanced drawing tools that can be added to
the drawing toolbar in EasyDraw™ and
PatchDraw. Refer to this section if you want to
know what each of the tools are used for, or if
you need to return to the default settings and
you can't remember what they are!

In EasyDraw™

Snap to Grid (turned ON by default)

The grid is made up of those tiny little dots that
you see when you are on the drawing board.
The number of dots is defined by our settings in
Drawing Board Setup. When Snap to Grid is
turned on, drawn lines will be attracted to these
dots or grid points like a magnet, in other
words, they "snap" into place. Most of your
drawing in EasyDraw™ will need to conform
to the grid setup to keep lines straight. You
would only need to turn Snap to Grid off if you
want your lines to snap to a node only or when
using Snap to Drawing.

Snap to Node (turned ON by default)

Nodes are the small black squares at the ends of
lines and arcs. With Snap to Node on, nodes
are attracted to one another in order to keep
your drawing "connected." Snap to Node can
be used alone or in conjunction with Snap to
Grid. You need to at least keep Snap to Node
on in order to prevent gaps or open spaces in
your drawing.

Snap to Drawing (turned OFF by default)

Use this feature when you want to control
where the lines snap to other lines and not to
the grid points or nodes. A node is created
wherever you park the drawn line or arc. This
is helpful when you need an odd angled line as
in a Crazy Patch block. *Only turn this tool on
when you need to use it,* and then turn it off
when you are done.

Snap to Grid

Define grid settings in Drawing Board Setup

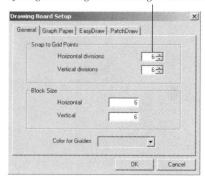

Snap to Node

Nodes are at the end of lines and arcs

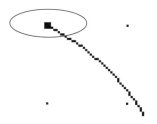

*Snap to Drawing
Only turn this tool on when
you need to use it, then turn it
off when you are done.*

Hide/Show Graph Paper

Hide/Show Graph Paper (turned ON by default)

If you have the graph paper set to "Graph paper lines" in Drawing Board Setup, you can easily turn them off and on by clicking on this tool.

In PatchDraw

Snap to Grid (turned OFF by default)

 Snap to Grid

Most of your drawing in PatchDraw will not need to conform to the grid setup, but sometimes you will want to draw something that does. With Snap to Grid turned on, lines and arcs and the pre-closed shapes will snap to the grid points when you draw them. Only end nodes and the initial drawing of closed shapes will snap to the grid points. Once drawn, the nodes of closed shapes can be moved without snapping to a grid point.

Snap to Node (turned ON by default)

 Snap to Node

This tool should be left on 99.9% of the time. It is rare that you would ever need to turn it off. Since PatchDraw must have closed shapes, this feature is there to help you draw them that way. The only time you may want to turn it off is if you are drawing two lines close together and you do not want the nodes to snap together.

Auto Align Similar Lines (turned ON by default)

 Auto Align Similar Lines

Similar lines and curves of separate shapes will snap to each other with this tool on. When you are placing shapes side by side that have similar lines or curves, you can choose whether or not you want your drawing to look like the shapes are sharing lines or nodes. For example, if you wanted a group of hexagons to look joined as in Grandmother's Flower Garden, you would want this tool on.

2

Snap Patch to Grid (turned OFF by default)

Snap Patch to Grid

With this tool on, shapes will snap to the grid points when you move them around or are drawing one of the pre-closed shapes. Although it looks like the entire shape is snapping into place, it is actually just one of the nodes. The node closest to a grid point when you release the mouse will be attracted. Having this tool on can help keep shapes aligned evenly when you want your appliqué drawing to be symmetrical.

Hide/Show Graph Paper (turned ON by default)

2

If you have the graph paper set to "Graph paper lines" in Drawing Board Setup, you can easily turn them off and on by clicking this tool.

Hide/Show Graph Paper

For the exercises in this chapter and beyond, make sure that you have added the advanced drawing tools for EasyDraw™ and PatchDraw to the drawing toolbar. (See pages 76 – 77 for instructions on "Adding the Advanced Drawing Features.") Once they are on the toolbar you can easily toggle them on and off. We may or may not use them for the exercises, but having them handy will be a real time saver.

Tip

- **For an overview on using the advanced drawing tools in EQ5, please take time to read pages 104 – 105 in the *EQ5 Design Cookbook*.**

- **Once you have turned the advanced drawing features on, you can also access the features in the BLOCK menu, Drawing Board Setup. Two new tabs, EasyDraw™ and PatchDraw, will have been added. Some of the features can be added to the drawing toolbars, others can only be accessed in the Drawing Board Setup.**

- **Begin the exercises in this chapter using the default settings for the tools. If you forget what the default settings are, refer to this section.**

- **Do not turn tools on or off until instructed to do so. Once you practice, by doing these exercises, you will understand more about how they work and will feel more comfortable using them.**

Drawing a Grandmother's Fan Block

Color blocks
on page 69

Grandmother's Fan
Block

Step 3
Arc Tool

Here's a popular block that we can draw to see how to use the Snap to Node tool by itself.

1   On the BLOCK menu, point to New Block, click EasyDraw™.

2   Also on the BLOCK menu, click Drawing Board Setup and enter these values:

General Tab
Snap to Grid Points
    Horizontal = 24   Vertical = 24
Block Size
    Horizontal = 6   Vertical = 6
Graph Paper Tab
Number of Divisions
    Horizontal = 6   Vertical = 6
Options
    Style = Graph paper lines

3   Click on the Arc tool.

⟍Tip

- **To make an arc flip in the opposite direction, press the Spacebar on your keyboard before releasing the mouse button.**

4   Draw an arc in the lower-left corner of the block, starting at 4.00" from the top of the block and ending it at 2.00" from the left side on the block outline.

Step 5

Step 6
Edit Tool

5   Draw a second larger arc, starting at 1/2" from the top of the block and ending at 5 1/2" from the left side on the block outline.

6   Click on the small black square in the corner of the Edit Tool to open the Edit Arc menu.

7   Click on the smaller arc to select it.

8   On the Edit Arc box, change the number beside Partition to 8.

Step 9
Click on the
Partition button

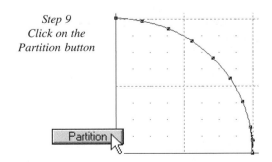

9   Click on the Partition button to add nodes and segment the arc into eight parts.

2

10 Click on the larger arc.

11 Click on the Partition button again to segment it into eight parts.

12 Click on the Line tool.

13 Click on the Snap to Grid button to turn it OFF. Turning off the Snap to Grid will prevent the lines from snapping to the grid points and make drawing this block much easier!

14 Click on the Snap to Node button to turn it ON.

15 Draw lines to connect the nodes between the smaller and larger arcs to create the fan blades. If you point the cursor right at the node, the line will be attracted to the node like a magnet.

16 Save your block in the Sketchbook. Click on the Color tab at the bottom of the screen and color your block as desired.

✎ **Tip**
• **Try some of your own fan blocks! Try partitioning the arcs in more segments or fewer segments than the one in the exercise. Remember to keep Snap to Grid turned ON when you draw the arcs, and turn it OFF when you draw the lines for the fan blades.**

Step 12
Line Tool   *Step 13*
Snap to Grid OFF   *Step 14*
Snap to Node ON

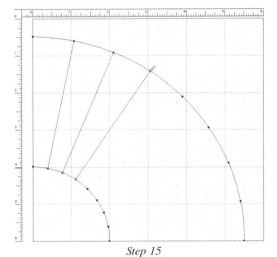

Step 15

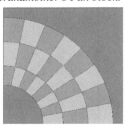

Completed Grandmother's Fan Block

Try these variations of the Grandmother's Fan block.

Add two more arcs. One 1/2" from the inside of the smaller arc, and one corner to corner, 1/2" away from the larger. Partition the two inner arcs.

Draw a new fan block with four arcs. Partition the smallest and largest arc and draw the straight lines to make the blades.

Drawing a Tilted Maple Leaf Block

Color blocks on page 70

*Step 3
Line Tool*

Tilted Maple Leaf Block

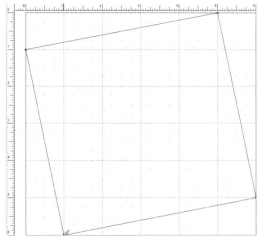

Step 4

*Step 5
Edit Tool*

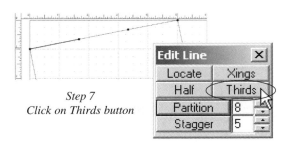

*Step 7
Click on Thirds button*

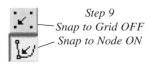

*Step 9
Snap to Grid OFF
Snap to Node ON*

Here's another block that makes use of partitioning and the Snap to Node tool.

1 On the BLOCK menu, point to New Block, click EasyDraw™.

2 Also on the BLOCK menu, click Drawing Board Setup and enter these values:

General Tab
Snap to Grid Points
Horizontal = 24   Vertical = 24
Block Size
Horizontal = 6   Vertical = 6
Graph Paper Tab
Number of Divisions
Horizontal = 6   Vertical = 6
Options
Style = Graph paper lines

3 Click on the Line tool.

4 Draw four lines to create a "tilted" square in the block. Begin 1.00" down from the top-left corner and end it at 5.00" from the left on the top of the block outline. Repeat until you have all four lines, beginning and ending each line 1.00" from the block corners.

5 Click on the small black square in the corner of the Edit Tool to open the Edit Line box.

6 Click on one of the tilted lines.

7 On the Edit Line box, click on Thirds to add nodes and segment the line into three parts. Repeat this step for each of the three remaining lines.

8 Click on the Line tool again.

9 Click on the Snap to Grid button to turn it OFF so that Snap to Node is the only tool enabled.

10 Draw lines to connect the nodes and make a Nine Patch grid in the tilted square.

11 Again, click on the small black square in the corner of the Edit Tool to open the Edit Line box.

12 Click on one of the tilted horizontal lines that you just drew, to select it.

13 On the Edit Line box, click on Xings. This creates nodes where the lines intersect.

14 Repeat the Xings with the other tilted horizontal line.

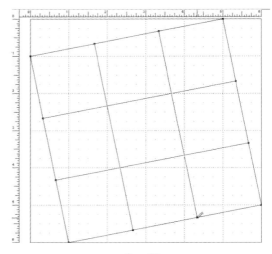

Step 10

✎ Tip

- **The Xings tool on the Edit Line/Arc box is very useful when you need to create nodes at intersections in your drawing without saving the block to the Sketchbook.**

15 Click on the Line tool.

16 Draw four diagonal lines as illustrated in the tilted Nine Patch, to form the leaf.

The stem is drawn in the lower-right grid square of the tilted Nine Patch, but we have to be a little creative in order to make it the correct size for our leaf.

17 Click on the small black square in the corner of the Edit tool again, to open the Edit Line box.

18 In the Edit Line box, change the number beside Partition to 8.

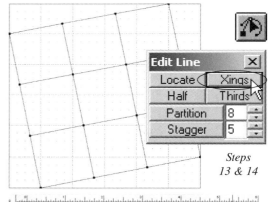

Steps 13 & 14

Step 16

This is the square you will draw the stem in.

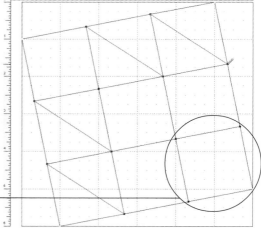

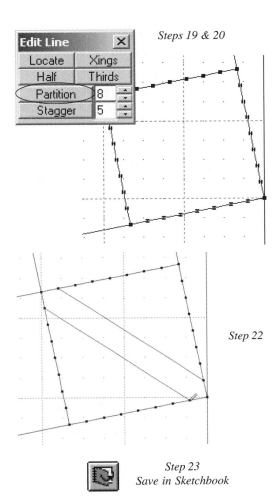

Steps 19 & 20

Step 22

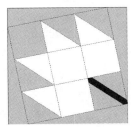

Step 23
Save in Sketchbook

19 Select one of the lines of the lower-right grid square and then click on Partition to segment the line into eight parts and add nodes.

20 Repeat this partitioning on each of the three remaining lines of the same grid square.

21 Click on the Line tool. Make sure that Snap to Grid is still turned OFF and Snap to Node is enabled.

22 Draw two diagonal lines for the stem as illustrated, using the nodes closest to the corners of the grid square.

23 Click on the Save in Sketchbook button to save your block.

✎ Tip ——————————————

• **This Tilted Maple Leaf looks great if you alternate the rotations on the quilt layout. It would make an interesting border treatment or just a quilt by itself.**

2

Try other tilted blocks. Try varying the tilt angle to get a different effect. How about a tilted pinwheel?

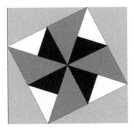

Completed Tilted
Maple Leaf Block

Example of a
Tilted Pinwheel Block

Drawing a Lone Star Block

*Color block
on page 70*

Here's that eight-point star again! This time we will transform it into the popular Lone Star block.

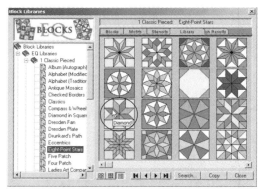

1 Retrieve the eight-point star named Diamond from the EQ Block Libraries under Classic Pieced, Eight-Point Stars. (See pages 32 – 33, steps 2 – 7, for details.) Click on the View Sketchbook button.

Step 1 Retrieve the eight-point star named Diamond.

2 In the Sketchbook, click on the Blocks tab.

3 On the Blocks tab, click to select the Diamond block.

4 Click the Edit button to place the Diamond block on the worktable. You don't need to change the Snap to Grid Points or Block Size.

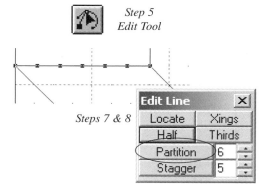

*Step 5
Edit Tool*

5 Click on the small black square in the corner of the Edit Tool to open the Edit Line box.

Steps 7 & 8

6 Click on any line to select it.

7 In the Edit Line box, change the number beside Partition to 6.

8 Click on the Partition button. This will divide the line into 6 segments.

9 Repeat this partitioning into 6 segments on all the star's lines.

Tip

• You cannot multiple select lines to do this, so you must partition each line of the diamond separately. You may find it helpful to move the Edit Line box. Do so by pointing to the top frame of the box and holding down the left mouse button to drag it as needed.

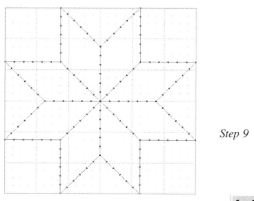

Step 9

10 Click on the Line tool.

11 Turn OFF all tools except Snap to Node.

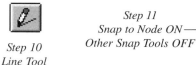

*Step 10
Line Tool*

*Step 11
Snap to Node ON
Other Snap Tools OFF*

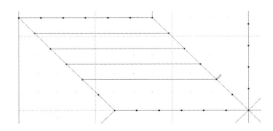

Step 12 Draw lines across Diamond to connect nodes

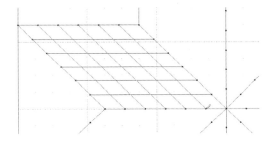

12 Draw lines to connect the nodes across each of the diamonds to make a 6 x 6 diamond grid.

Tip

• **You may find it helpful to use the Zoom tool when drawing the lines within each diamond.**

• **To see the nodes when you retrieve a block from the Sketchbook and place it on the worktable, use the Select tool and click twice on any line in the block. Don't double click, but click on a line to select it and then click on it again after a brief pause. If you accidentally move the line out of place use Undo (CTRL+Z) to move it back.**

13 Click on the Save in Sketchbook button to save your block.

2

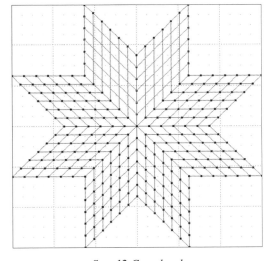

Step 12 Completed

*Completed
Lone Star Block*

Drawing a Random String-Pieced Star

*Color blocks
on pages 70 – 71*

The Snap to Drawing tool is used when you
want to connect a line to another line at any
point. When the Snap to Drawing tool is
enabled, and all other advanced drawing tools
are turned off, the drawn line will be attracted to
existing lines in the block or to the block
outline. A node will appear on the existing line
(except for the block outline) wherever you
park the line.

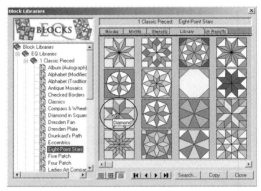

✎ Tip

- **Always remember to turn OFF the Snap to
Drawing tool when you are done using it! For
most drawing in EasyDraw™ you will not need
it, and you would not normally want lines
snapping to other lines. Snap to Grid and Snap
to Node are on by default.**

Step 1 Retrieve the eight-point star named Diamond.

1   Retrieve the eight-point star named
    Diamond from the Block Libraries under
    Classic Pieced, Eight-Point Stars. (See
    pages 32 – 33, steps 2 – 7, for details.)
    Click on the View Sketchbook button.

2   In the Sketchbook, click on the Blocks tab.

3   On the Blocks tab, click to select the
    Diamond block.

4   Click Edit to place the Diamond block on
    the worktable. You do not need to change
    the Snap to Grid Points or Block Size.

5   Click on the Line tool.

6   Click on the Snap to Drawing button to
    turn it ON. Turn Snap to Grid, Snap to
    Node, and the Hide/Show Graph Paper
    buttons OFF.

7   Point the cursor directly at any line in the
    block and draw a line to the other side of
    the diamond and release the mouse. The
    drawn line is attracted to the existing line
    and a node is created wherever you release
    the mouse button. If you miss the line or
    don't like the placement, use Undo
    (CTRL+Z) immediately and redraw the line.

*Step 6
Snap to Grid OFF
Snap to Node OFF
Snap to Drawing ON
Hide/Show Graph Paper OFF*

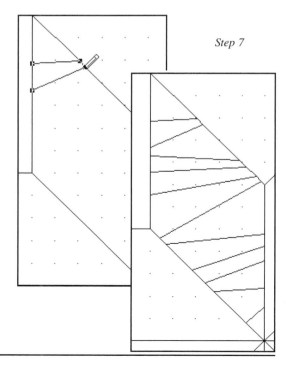

Step 7

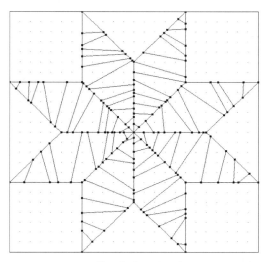

Step 8 Completed

8 Continue drawing lines across the diamonds until you have them all filled with strings. Strings (representing strips of fabric) can be thin or thick. The lines do not have to be parallel. This is supposed to be somewhat random, so don't worry if your lines aren't perfectly straight.

Once you get used to the freedom of drawing lines with this tool, you can go really fast. It's just like you were drawing lines with a pencil. All you have to do is stay in the lines. Actually, it's much easier to do this in EQ5 than on paper!

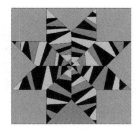

Completed Random String-Pieced Star

You can make just about any block into a string-piecing type block. Try these blocks and then experiment with some of your own.

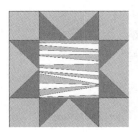

Variation 1

Variation 2

2

Drawing a Crazy Patch Star Block

 Color block on page 71

Drawing crazy patch also uses the Snap to Drawing tool. Let's try it on the Diamond Star.

1 Retrieve the eight-point star named Diamond from the Block Libraries under Classic Pieced, Eight-Point Stars. (See pages 32 – 33, steps 2 – 7, for details.)

2 On the Blocks tab of the Sketchbook, click to select the Diamond block.

3 Click the Edit button to place the Diamond block on the worktable. You don't need to change the Snap to Grid Points or Block Size.

4 Click on the Line tool.

5 Click on the Snap to Drawing button to turn it ON. Turn the Snap to Grid, Snap to Node, and Hide/Show Graph Paper buttons OFF.

6 Point to any line in the star and draw a line from one side of the diamond to the other. The lines for crazy patch are very random, but your lines must be drawn between two existing lines so they will have something to snap to. Try subdividing the diamond into sections first, then subdivide the sections further.

7 Continue drawing lines between lines until you have filled the diamond with a crazy patch design.

8 Repeat this random crazy patch drawing in the remaining diamonds. Try to vary the line placement to make your star really crazy!

9 Click on the Save in Sketchbook button.

We used an eight-point star block for this exercise, but any block with a large open patch will work equally well. Select a block and go crazy with it!

*Step 4
Line Tool*

*Step 5
Snap to Grid OFF
Snap to Node OFF
Snap to Drawing ON
Hide/Show Graph Paper OFF*

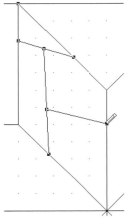
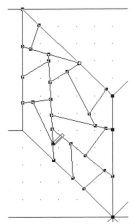

Step 6   *Step 6 Completed*

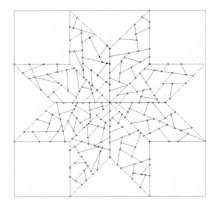
Step 9 Completed

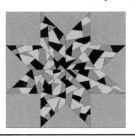
*Completed Crazy
Patch Star Block*

Drawing Folk Art Tulips in PatchDraw
*Color block
on page 72*

*Step 3
Snap to Grid ON
Snap to Node ON
Auto Align Similar Lines OFF
Snap Patch to Grid ON
Hide/Show Graph Paper ON*

*Step 4
Simple Oval Fly-out*

*Step 5
Curved Leaf*

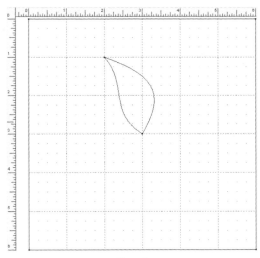

Step 6

*Step 7
Bezier Edit Tool*

Folk art tulips are probably the second most used flower in appliqué designs. (Roses are the most popular.) Use the advanced drawing tools to help you keep their petals symmetrical. Our goal in this exercise is to create several tulip tops to save in the User Libraries to be used in other projects.

1   On the BLOCK menu, point to New Block, click PatchDraw.

2   Also on the BLOCK menu, click Drawing Board Setup and enter these values:
   General Tab
   Snap to Grid Points
       Horizontal = 24   Vertical = 24
   Block Size
       Horizontal = 6   Vertical = 6
   Graph Paper Tab
   Number of Divisions
       Horizontal = 6   Vertical = 6
   Options
       Style = Graph paper lines

3   Click on the Snap to Grid, Snap to Node and Snap Patch to Grid to turn them ON. Turn the Auto-Align button OFF.

4   Click on the small black triangle on the Simple Oval tool to open the fly-out.

5   Click on the curved leaf shape, the fifth shape from the left on the fly-out.

6   Point the cursor at any graph paper line intersection and drag the mouse downward to the right about one inch away to make a leaf that's about 2.00" tall. It does not have to be exact.

7   Click on the the small black square in the corner of the Bezier Edit tool to open the Edit Node box.

8   Click on the leaf's bottom node.

2

9 On the Edit Node box, click on Break to separate the nodes at the bottom. You will now have two end nodes.

10 When separated, one node will remain selected, shown by the handle extending from it. Drag this node so it is 1" to the right and 1/2" down from the top node.

Notice how with Snap to Grid on, the end nodes snap to a grid point. This is helpful when trying to create a symmetrical shape.

11 Click on the top curve so that you can see both handles. Drag the handles, adjusting them to make a smooth curve.

12 Click on the bottom curve and drag the handle to the left to widen the tulip a little.

⟍ Tip ⎯⎯⎯⎯⎯⎯⎯⎯⎯⎯⎯⎯⎯

- **If the bottom node is not resting on a grid point, drag it until it snaps into place, keeping it lined up with the top-center node.**

13 Click on the small black square in the corner of the Select tool to open the Symmetry box.

14 Click on the tulip half, to select it

15 On the Symmetry box, click on Clone.

16 With the shape still selected, click Flip H.

17 Drag the new half to join up with the original half. With Snap Patch to Grid on, it will snap into place.

At this point, while the two halves are still not joined, check to see if you are happy with the tulip's shape. If you feel it needs adjusting, mentally note where, then select and delete the new half. Make your adjustments to the first half only. This will keep the tulip symmetrical. Repeat steps 15 and 16 when adjustments are complete. Move the new half into place.

18 Click on the Bezier Edit tool.

Step 9

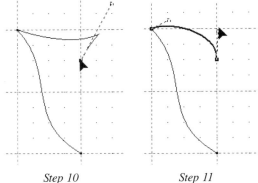

Step 10 *Step 11*

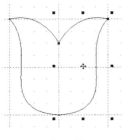

Step 12

Steps 15 & 16

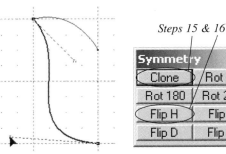

Step 17

Step 18
Bezier Edit Tool

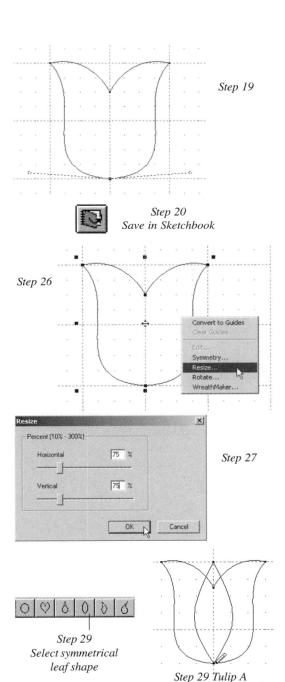

Step 19

Step 20
Save in Sketchbook

Step 26

Step 27

Step 29
Select symmetrical
leaf shape

Step 29 Tulip A
leaf shape on top of tulip

19 Click on the center top and bottom nodes to join them. With PatchDraw's Auto-join feature, one click is usually all it takes. Two handles will appear when the nodes are joined.

20 Click on Save in Sketchbook.

Now that you have saved this first tulip shape, let's try some other options to learn how one shape can be used for several different styles.

21 Click on the Select tool and then click on the tulip to select it.

22 Click on the Copy button (CTRL+C).

23 On the BLOCK menu, point to New Block, click PatchDraw.

24 Click on the Paste button (CTRL+V). We now have the original tulip on a new PatchDraw block. We will create six different tulip top styles using this same shape on one block.

25 Select the tulip shape and right-click on it to bring up the context menu.

26 On the context menu, click on Resize.

27 In the Resize box, type in 75 for both the Horizontal and Vertical percentages and click OK.

28 The resized tulip shape is selected. Drag it to the upper-left corner of the block.

29 **Tulip A**. Select, copy, and paste the resized tulip shape (Steps 21 – 24). Click on the symmetrical leaf shape on the Simple Oval tool fly-out. Draw a leaf shape, beginning slightly above the center of the tulip and ending at the bottom node of the tulip. Adjust the curve of the leaf with the Bezier Edit tool if desired. This creates a two layered effect as seen in many folk art appliqué designs.

2

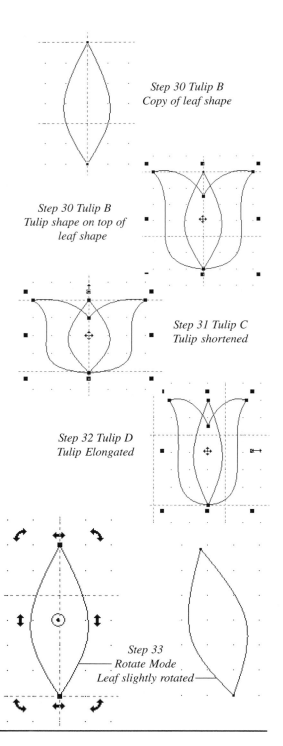

Tip

- **To see all the adjustment handles at once, hold down the SHIFT key and click on both curves of the leaf. This will help you keep the leaf symmetrical when you adjust the handles.**

30 Tulip B. First, copy the leaf shape created with Tulip A and paste it in a new location on the block. Next, copy and paste the tulip shape. Move the tulip shape over the leaf. It will look the same as Tulip A, but this one will have the tulip shape in front.

31 Tulip C. Copy and paste Tulip B. Click on the Select tool and drag a selection box around the tulip to include both parts. Point the cursor at the top center handle of the selection box around the tulip and drag it down to make a shorter tulip.

32 Tulip D. Copy and paste Tulip B. Select both parts as before, but this time adjust the width to make a tall and narrow tulip.

33 Tulip E. Copy and paste the leaf shape. While holding down the CTRL key, click on the crossed arrows in the center of the leaf to go into rotate mode. Rotate the leaf slightly to the left by dragging the curved arrow in the corner of the leaf shape in the direction you want to rotate.

Step 30 Tulip B
Copy of leaf shape

Step 30 Tulip B
Tulip shape on top of leaf shape

Step 31 Tulip C
Tulip shortened

Step 32 Tulip D
Tulip Elongated

Step 33
Rotate Mode
Leaf slightly rotated

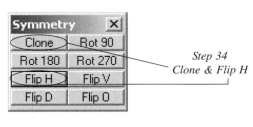

Step 34
Clone & Flip H

34 Click on the small black square in the corner of the Select tool to open the Symmetry box. Click Clone, then click Flip H to make a mirror image. Turn OFF Snap Patch to Grid and drag the flipped leaf so it overlaps the first one and the bottom nodes match up.

35 Copy and paste a new leaf and center it over the previous pair.

36 Copy and paste the tulip shape and move it so that it is centered over the previous leaf-shaped layers. This creates a three dimensional tulip.

37 Click on the Save in Sketchbook button to save your block.

2

\ Tip ————————————————————

• **Save your tulip collection block in the User Libraries so that you can easily access the tulip to use on other projects. See pages 14 – 17 for directions.**

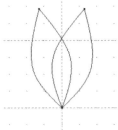
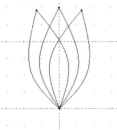

Step 34
Move second leaf until
nodes match up

Step 35
Copy another leaf &
center it over
previous pair

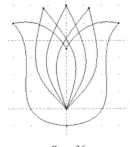
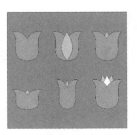

Step 36

Folk Art Tulips

Try other tulip shapes and alternative styles. Make a whole collection of blocks to keep in your User Libraries to easily access in other projects. Here are a few examples.

Creating a Folk Art Tulip Wreath

Color block
on page 72

This exercise is meant to be used in conjuction with the Folk Art Tulips that were created in the previous exercise. If you did not complete the tulip exercise, do so now so that you will have the appliqué shapes to use in the wreath.

Step 5
Select Tool

1   From the User Libraries, copy one or more of the blocks containing the tulip tops created in the previous exercise. (Pages 124 – 125 in the *EQ5 Design Cookbook*.)

2   Click on the View Sketchbook button and click on the Blocks tab.

3   Click on the block containing the tulip top you want to use in your wreath.

4   Click on the Edit button. The block will be on the worktable now.

5   Click on the Select tool.

6   Point to the drawing board and drag a selection box around a tulip to select the design that you want to use in the wreath, or hold down the SHIFT key and click on each part.

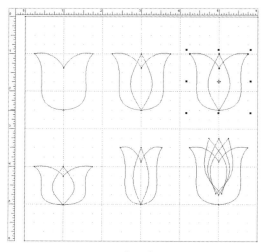

Step 6

7   Click on the Copy button.

8   On the BLOCK menu, point to New Block, click PatchDraw.

9   Click on the Paste button to place the tulip design on the new block. *While the tulip is still selected*, move it to the center near the top of the block. (The size of your tulip will probably vary from the illustration.) Resize your tulip shape if necessary to keep the height under 2.00".

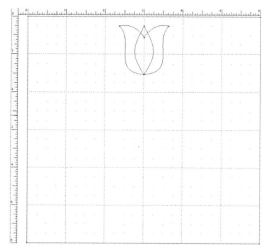

Step 9

Step 11
Snap to Grid
Snap to Node
Snap Patch to Grid
Tools ON

Steps 12 & 13
Rectangle Shape

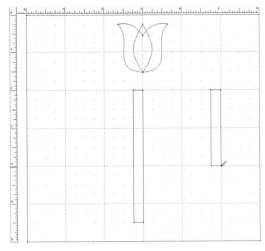

Step 14

At this point, we need to change the Snap to Grid points in order to complete this block. When you copy a part of a block from the library and paste it on a new block, the drawing board will have the same setup as the old block. You may discover you need to change the snap points to accommodate your new drawing. This is perfectly alright and reminds you of how versatile PatchDraw can be.

10 Also on the BLOCK menu, click Drawing Board Setup and enter these values:

General Tab
Snap to Grid Points
    Horizontal = 48   Vertical = 48
Block Size
    Horizontal = 6   Vertical = 6
Graph Paper Tab
Number of Divisions
    Horizontal = 6   Vertical = 6
Options
    Style = Graph paper lines

11 Click on Snap to Grid, Snap to Node, and Snap Patch to Grid tools to turn them ON.

12 Click on the small black arrow in the corner of the Simple shapes tool to open the fly-out menu.

13 Click on the rectangle shape. It's the last shape on the fly-out.

14 Click and drag the mouse diagonally from left to right, draw a 1/4" wide vertical stem that is 3" to 3 1/2" tall. Draw a second stem 1 1/2" to 2" tall in another area of the block. The height does not have to be exact, but you need to keep them 1/4" wide. With Snap to Grid on, this should be very easy.

15 Click on the Select tool.

2

16 Click on the longer stem to select it and move it until it is centered under the tulip, overlapping it slightly.

17 Point to the drawing board and drag a selection box around the tulip top to select it, or hold down the SHIFT key and click on each part. Make sure you do NOT select the stem.

18 Click on the Copy button.

19 Click on the Paste button to place another tulip top on the block. While the tulip is still selected, move it so that it is centered over the shorter stem, overlapping it slightly.

20 Hold down the SHIFT key and click on the shorter stem. All parts of the second tulip top and short stem should now be selected. Right-click on the drawing board to bring up the PatchDraw context menu.

21 Click on Rotate.

22 In the Rotate box, type in 60 for the degrees of rotation. Click OK.

23 With the rotated stem still selected, move it over and place it so that it's about halfway down the first stem. Be sure to overlap it so that the bottom of the stem is entirely *inside the width* of the first stem. Since Snap Patch to Grid is enabled, the nodes will snap to the nearest grid point. Play with the placement and find what works best.

24 Click on the small black square in the corner of the Select tool or by right-clicking on the drawing board to open the Symmetry box.

25 Click on the shorter stem to select it and then on the click on the Clone button in Symmetry box.

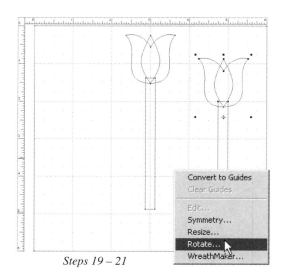

Steps 19 – 21

Step 22

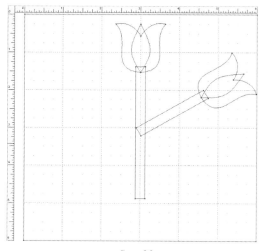

Step 23

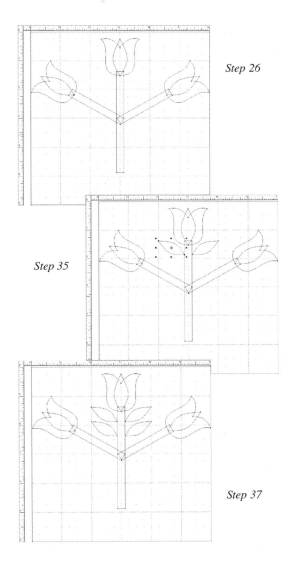

Step 26

Step 35

Step 37

26 With the cloned stem still selected, click on Flip H. Move this stem and place it opposite the first one.

27 Click on the small black arrow in the corner of the Simple Oval tool to open the fly-out. Click on the vertical leaf shape (fourth from the left).

28 In another area of the block, draw a leaf 1.00" tall. (For the leaves of my tulip wreath, I took a shortcut and copied the center part of my tulip and then reduced the size.)

29 Click on the Select tool.

30 Click on the leaf to select it.

31 With the leaf selected, right-click on the drawing board to bring up the context menu and then click on Rotate.

32 In the Rotate box, type in 60 for the degrees of rotation and then click OK.

33 With the rotated leaf still selected, move it over to the right side of the center stem and place it under the tulip head. Overlap the stem, let it rest along the edge, or leave a space depending on the effect you want.

34 If the Symmetry box is not open, click on the small black square on the Select tool or right-click on the drawing board to open it.

35 With the leaf still selected, click on Clone and then click on Flip H on the Symmetry box. Move the new leaf to the opposite side of the stem so that it is even with the first leaf. Click off the leaf to de-select it.

36 To make a second set of leaves identical to the first, hold down the SHIFT key and click on the leaves to select them both.

37 Click on Clone and move the new set beneath the first set of leaves. Click off the leaves to de-select them.

2

38 To easily make a pair of leaves for the other tulip branches, hold down the SHIFT key and select the two leaves on the *right side of the stem*. On the Symmetry box, click on Clone.

39 With the cloned leaves still selected, right-click, choose Rotate and rotate them 60 degrees. Unless you made a change, EQ5 will remember the last number you typed in for the degrees. Move the new leaves to the bottom of the right tulip branch.

40 To make an identical pair of leaves for the opposite branch, click on Clone and then on Flip H on the Symmetry box. Move the new leaves below the left tulip branch.

Step 40

Tip

• **You can save your tulip "branches" at any point as you are building them in PatchDraw. This makes it easy to retrieve the block later and make changes, or to make an entirely different design using the same base.**

Now let's make a heart base for this tulip branch. The heart will create a petal type center when we make a wreath out of it.

41 On the Simple Oval tool fly-out, click on the heart shape.

42 Draw a heart shape at the base of the center stem. When you drag out the heart shape, follow the vertical line of the center graph paper line to keep it symmetrical as you draw.

43 Once you have the heart drawn, you can click on the select tool and drag the nodes to resize it. Keep the width and height around 2.00". Your design may vary.

Step 41
Simple Oval Tool Fly-out
Heart Shape

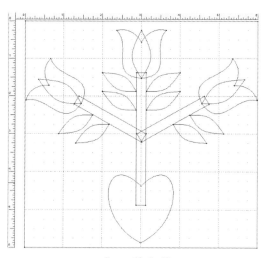

Steps 42 & 43

Step 44
Bezier Edit Tool

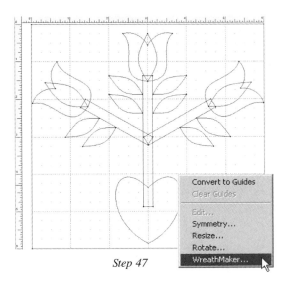

Step 47

Step 48

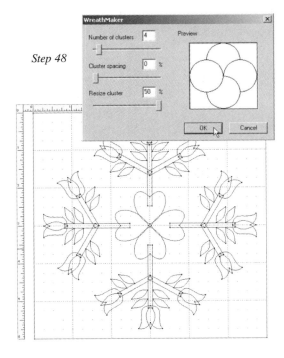

44 Use the Bezier Edit tool to adjust the curves of the heart if desired. Once you edit the heart, select it again and move it back to the center if needed. With the Snap Patch to Grid feature on, it should go right back into place.

45 Click on Save in Sketchbook to save the appliqué design at this point BEFORE we make a wreath out of it.

46 After the tulip branch is saved to the Sketchbook, draw a selection box to include the entire tulip branch without the block outline. You may find it easier to use Select All on the EDIT menu (CTRL+A), but remember this will include the block outline in the selection. Hold down the SHIFT key and click on the block outline to de-select it.

47 Right-click on the drawing board and click on WreathMaker.

48 In the WreathMaker box, in Number of clusters, type 4. Under the Cluster spacing, first try 0% spacing (slide the bar all the way to the left) to keep the hearts close together in the center. Under Cluster size, try sliding the bar all the way to the right. If your original design fills the block, the percentage will probably not go much past 50%. Click OK.

There is a bit of trial and error here, but your aim should be to get the hearts in the center as close as possible without having them overlap. If the first try doesn't work, click on CTRL+Z to undo (also on the EDIT menu) *immediately*, get back to the WreathMaker box and try adjusting the Cluster spacing to the right in small amounts.

2

49 Once you are happy with your wreath, click on Save in Sketchbook to save it. Use the circle on the Simple Oval tool fly-out to add a flower center to your design if you like.

Keeping on Top of Things in PatchDraw

Generally, when drawing an appliqué design in PatchDraw, we try to draw the bottom layer first so that it will be layered correctly when we color the block. However, sometimes that just isn't possible, especially if we are building a block from copied parts of another block. Here's a little trick to keep your layers in order.

1 Hold down the SHIFT key and using the Select tool, select the patches in the block that need to be on the top layer.

2 Click on Copy button (CTRL+C) to copy your selected patches.

3 While the patches still selected, right-click and choose Convert to Guides.

4 Click on the Paste button (CTRL+V). Move the newly pasted patches into place using the guidelines for exact placement.

Now they are on top!

Tip

• **You can layer using this trick when you are on the PatchDraw tab, or you can layer your patches from the Color tab using Send to Front and Send to Back. Just remember the PatchDraw background square is also a patch and needs to be sent to back if you change any layering.**

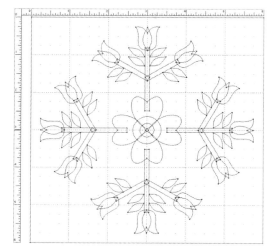

Step 49

Step 2
Copy Tool

Step 4
Paste Tool

Completed Folk Art
Tulip Wreath

Drawing Blocks for Prairie Point Borders

Step 3
Snap to Grid
Snap to Node
Auto Align Similar Lines
Snap Patch to Grid
ALL ON

Steps 4 & 5

Half Square Triangle

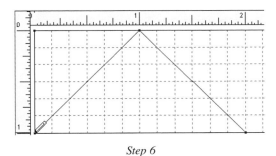

Step 6

Step 7
Select Tool

EQ5 gives us the unique ability to add borders that can extend over the edge of the quilt. We can use the advanced drawing features to create sets of prairie points that we can use to simulate these triangular points. You will find this very helpful when you are trying to figure out how many prairie points you will need!

1   On the BLOCK menu, point to New Block, click PatchDraw.

2   Also on the BLOCK menu, click Drawing Board Setup and enter these values:

General Tab
Snap to Grid Points
    Horizontal = 36   Vertical = 6
Block Size
    Horizontal = 6   Vertical = 1
Graph Paper Tab
Number of Divisions
    Horizontal = 36   Vertical = 6
Options
    Style = Graph paper lines

3   Click the Snap to Grid, Snap to Node, Auto Align Similar Lines and Snap Patch to Grid tools ON.

4   Click on the small black triangle in the corner of the Simple Shape tool to open the fly-out.

5   Click on the half square triangle (the first on the fly-out).

6   Point the cursor at the top of the block 1.00" from the left and drag the mouse diagonally back to the lower-left corner to create a triangle with the larger side at the bottom. With all the tools on, the triangle will snap right into place when you release the mouse. The bottom of the triangle will be 2.00" long.

7   Click on the Select tool.

2

8 Click on the triangle to select it.

9 Click on the Copy button.

10 Click on the Paste button.

11 While the copied triangle is still selected, move it to the right so that the lower-left point is touching the first triangle. Again, it will snap right into place.

12 Click on the Copy button.

13 Click on the Paste button.

14 While the copied triangle is still selected, drag it to the right so that you have three triangles end to end across the block.

15 You will need to make your prairie points a free floating motif to be able to use it for a virtual border on a quilt worktable. Click on the block outline to select it. Press your keyboard DELETE key.

16 Click on the Save in Sketchbook button to save your block.

Steps 9 & 12
Copy Button

Steps 10 & 13
Paste Button

Step 14

Step 15
No Block Outline

Step 16
Save in Sketchbook

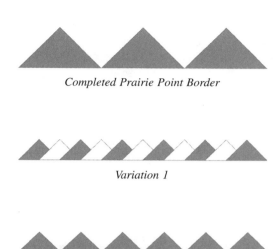

Completed Prairie Point Border

Variation 1

Variation 2

Variation 3

Variation 4

Prairie Point Border

Sample Prairie Point Sets

This exercise created a block with only three prairie points across. You can of course make more points across the block and overlap them if needed – just like real prairie points. Keep in mind that the long side of prairie point triangles is twice the height. Use the same drawing board setup to create the sets to the left.

Tip

- Creating your prairie points in sets makes them easier to draw. The smaller size allows them to be used on varying quilt sizes.

- Set your prairie points on the quilt edge of Layer 2 and use the Graph Pad to fine tune the size and placement. Click on the Fit to Window button after placing a block to keep the virtual border visible. Use the handy Copy and Paste tools on the quilt worktable to quickly place several sets along the quilt edges. Rotate and resize as needed.

- If you want to create a set of prairie points that overlap, you will need to increase or decrease the Horizontal size of the block and adjust the snap points accordingly.

- Prairie point blocks can be resized on the quilt worktable using the Graph Pad. Keep the size proportional if you can. If you need to lengthen or shorten the block slightly, this is perfectly alright, since this is just a virtual border. Even if small adjustments are made, you can still get an approximate count for the number of prairie points you will need to fit your particular quilt.

2

Drawing Blocks for Scalloped Borders

A scalloped edge border can transform a plain quilt into a fancy one. We can use EQ5 to create scalloped border blocks with ease!

1   On the BLOCK menu, point to New Block, click PatchDraw.

2   Also on the BLOCK menu, click Drawing Board Setup and enter these values:

General Tab
Snap to Grid Points
     Horizontal = 32   Vertical = 6
Block Size
     Horizontal = 16   Vertical = 3
Graph Paper Tab
Number of Divisions
     Horizontal = 16   Vertical = 3
Options
     Style = Graph paper lines

3   Click the Snap to Grid, Snap to Node and Snap Patch to Grid tools ON. Having Auto Align Similar Lines on or off will not affect the drawing of this block.

4   Click on the Bezier tool.

5   Beginning 1.00" down from the top-left corner of the block, draw a horizontal curve that is 4.00" long. The end nodes will snap to the grid.

6   Click on the Bezier Edit tool. Click on the curve to select it.

7   Drag the handles so that the curve is even. Place the handles on top of the block an equal distance from the top-left corner and the 4.00" line.

8   Click on the Select tool. Click on the curve to select it.

9   Click on the Copy button.

10   Click on the Paste button.

Step 3
Snap to Grid ON
Snap to Node ON
Auto Align Similar Lines OFF
Snap Patch to Grid ON

Step 4
Bezier Tool

Step 5

Step 6
Bezier Edit Tool

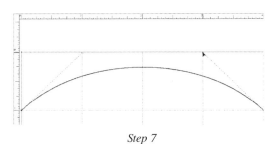

Step 7

Step 8
Select Tool

Step 9
Copy Button

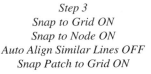

Step 10
Paste Button

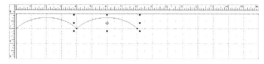

Step 11

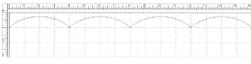

Step 12

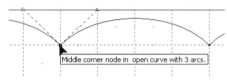

Middle corner node in open curve with 3 arcs.

Step 14
After three arcs have been joined,
fourth arc still needs to be joined

Step 17
Line Tool

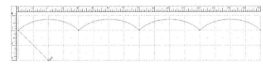

Step 18

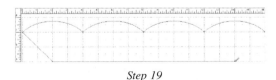

Step 19

Step 20

11 Drag the copied scallop over to the right so it is lined up with the first one and the end nodes meet. With Snap Patch to Grid on, the scallop will snap into place.

12 Repeat this copy and paste (Steps 9 & 10) two more times until you have four scallops end to end across the block.

13 Click on the Bezier Edit tool.

14 Point and click on the nodes between the scallops. The Auto-join feature will join the nodes since they are on top of one another.

Tip

- There are two ways to determine if the nodes are joined when you click on them as in Step 14. One, the tooltip message will change from "Final node in open curve..." to "Middle corner node in open curve..." And two, when you click on the node, two handles will appear at the node instead of one.

Now you have a row of four even scallops, but we're not done yet. We have to make the scallops into a closed shape.

15 Click on the Select tool.

16 Click on the block outline to select it. Then press your keyboard DELETE key to delete it.

17 Click on the Line tool.

18 Draw a diagonal line. Begin at the node on the left end of the scallops and end at the bottom of the block 2.00" from the left side.

19 Still using the Line tool, draw a horizontal line across the bottom of the block. Begin at the end node of the diagonal line and end at 14.00".

20 Draw a diagonal line from the end node of the bottom line to the end node of the far right scallop to complete the closed shape.

2

Tip

- **If you began and ended the line right on the nodes your shape should be closed. You can double check by clicking on the Bezier Edit tool and point without clicking over one of the nodes and read the tooltip. If the tooltip message says that the curve is still open, the culprit nodes are probably one of the last ones drawn. You can easily join them using the Bezier Edit tool by dragging one on top of the other.**

- **It's important that you have a 45 degree line for the ends of the scallop block so that it will fit around the corners of the quilt correctly. The resulting angle will simulate a mitered corner.**

If you are not sure of the size to draw your scalloped border blocks, go to the quilt worktable first. Add a mitered border to the quilt the approximate width desired. Determine the size of the mitered border and subtract 2.00" (to allow for the scalloped corners which are 1.00" from the corners).

22 Click on the Save in Sketchbook button to save your block.

This 16.00" x 3.00" scallop block will fit around a quilt with a 12.00" quilt center. If you increase or decrease the size of the quilt center, increase or decrease the size of the scallop block proportionally.

Now that you have the basic idea, you can try another approach for designing scalloped border blocks. Since we don't always have a quilt center that is even, we can draw two different scalloped border blocks, one for the corners and one for the center. The blocks are both 8.00" x 3.00". Making separate blocks shown here will make them more versatile.

You can simulate binding on your scalloped border blocks by layering two shapes, one on top of the other. Adjust the top layer slightly to reveal the bottom layer.

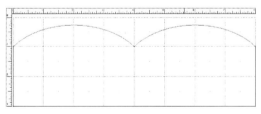

Using the Bezier Edit Tool, place cursor over the node to see if you have an open or closed shape.

Middle corner node in closed curve with 7 arcs.

Completed Scalloped Border

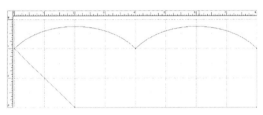

Variation Corner

Variation Side

Completed Variation Border

Drawing Geometric Border Stencils

Step 3
Snap to Grid ON
Snap to Node ON
Auto Align Similar Lines OFF
Snap Patch to Grid ON

Step 4
Select Tool

Step 5
Simple Shape fly-out
60 degree diamond

Need a quick and easy border stencil? EQ5 can help!

1 On the BLOCK menu, point to New Block, click PatchDraw.

2 Also on the BLOCK menu, click Drawing Board Setup and enter these values:

General Tab
Snap to Grid Points
    Horizontal = 24   Vertical = 8
Block Size
    Horizontal = 24   Vertical = 4
Graph Paper Tab
Number of Divisions
    Horizontal = 24   Vertical = 8
Options
    Style = Graph paper lines

3 Click the Snap to Grid, Snap to Node and Snap Patch to Grid tools ON. Having Auto Align Similar Lines on or off will not affect the drawing of this block.

We'll begin by creating a diamond cable stencil and then see some other shapes you can use in the same way.

Before drawing, let's remove the block outline. Since we are making a border stencil, we don't need the block outline. The graph paper lines will still be on the drawing board to guide you.

4 Click the Select tool. Click on the block outline to select it, and then press your keyboard DELETE key.

5 Click on the small black triangle in the corner of the Simple Shape tool to open the fly-out. Click on the 60 degree diamond, the fourth shape from left on the fly-out.

6 Beginning 1.50" from the top of the block on the left side, draw a diamond that is 4.00" wide.

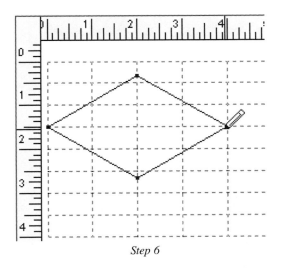

Step 6

2

7 Click on the Select tool.

8 Click on the diamond to select it.

9 Click on the Copy button.

10 Click on the Paste button.

11 Drag the copied diamond to overlap the first one so the left point is 2.50" from the block top on the left side. The overlapped shapes should be centered vertically.

12 Using the Select tool, draw a select box around the two diamonds to select them, or hold down the keyboard SHIFT key and click on each diamond to select both.

13 Click on the Copy button.

14 Click on the Paste button.

15 Drag the copied pair of diamonds to the right of the first pair so the points are touching. With Snap Patch to Grid on, they will snap right into place.

16 Repeat this copy and paste (Steps 13 & 14) until you have six pairs of diamonds end to end across the block.

17 Click on the Save in Sketchbook button to save your block.

Do you see the diamond cable now? Click on the Hide/Show Graph Paper tool to turn the graph paper lines off temporarily so you can see your stencil more clearly.

Creating a diamond cable like the one in this exercise results in an open-ended cable. You can create shorter blocks and use repeats to fit any border size. But what if you want a cable to end with a closed diamond? We can do that too!

Step 9
Copy Button

Step 10
Paste Button

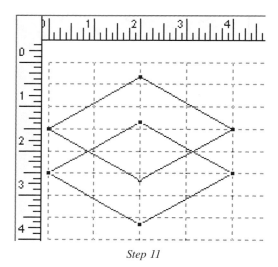

Step 11

Step 15

Hide/Show Graph Paper Tool

Completed Geometric Border
Graph Paper lines turned OFF

Step 3
60 degree diamond

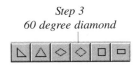

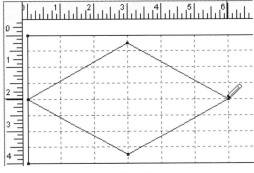

Step 4

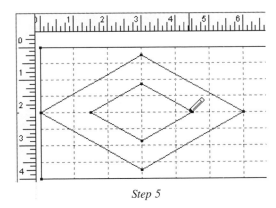

Step 5

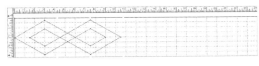

Step 9

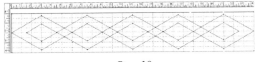

Step 10

1   On the BLOCK menu, point to New Block, click PatchDraw.

2   Also on the BLOCK menu, click Drawing Board Setup and enter these values:
    General Tab
    Snap to Grid Points
        Horizontal = 48   Vertical = 8
    Block Size
        Horizontal = 24   Vertical = 4
    Graph Paper Tab
    Number of Divisions
        Horizontal = 24   Vertical = 4
    Options
        Style = Graph paper lines

3   Click on the small black triangle in the corner of the Simple Shape tool. Click on the 60 degree diamond, the fourth shape from the left on the fly-out.

4   Beginning 2.00" from the top on the left side of the block draw a diamond that is 6.00" and is centered vertically on the block.

5   Draw another smaller diamond inside the first one. To make a 3.00" diamond, begin at 1.50" from the left and end at 4.50".

6   Click on the Select tool. Hold down the keyboard SHIFT key and click on each diamond.

7   Click on the Copy button.

8   Click on the Paste button.

9   Drag the copied diamonds to the right of the first set, overlapping them 1.00", so the points of the large and small diamonds are touching. With Snap Patch to Grid on, it will snap right into place.

10 Repeat this copy and paste (Steps 7 & 8) to have five diamond sets across the block.

2

11 Delete the block outline, then click on the Save in Sketchbook button.

\Tip ──────────────
- **Don't color that stencil! If you colored the block it would not look like a stencil at all, but would look like rows of solid diamonds.**

Here are some examples of other shapes and the border designs you can make from them. The six-sided shape is the hexagon on the Simple Polygon tool. Right-click and use the Resize option to reduce the Vertical size to 75 percent.

\Tip ──────────────
- **When you save a block to the Sketchbook without the block outline, it will be saved on the Motifs tab. You can move the block to the Stencils tab in the Sketchbook or in the Blocks palette or the quilt worktable. Near the top of the Sketchbook or the Blocks palette, click on the small arrow button. On this menu, click on Move to Tab and then click on Stencils Tab.**

- **You may notice that your border stencil looks really squished when viewed in the Sketchbook and the Blocks palette. This is normal since all blocks are viewed as squares. Use the Notecard in the Sketchbook to give your border stencils a unique name that will help you easily identify them. To get a larger view of the block, you can change the number of blocks viewed in both the Sketchbook and the Blocks palette. You can also resize the Blocks palette by pointing to an edge and dragging it when you see the double-headed arrow appears.**

- **Save your stencils in the User Libraries so that you can use them in other projects. See pages 14 – 17 for directions.**

To make a corner stencil that will match up with long border stencils, draw it on a square block with the size the same as the height of your border stencil *or* draw it on the same block. Use corresponding Snap to Grid Points and Graph Paper Divisions. For instance, if the diamond border cable block is 16.00" x 4.00", make the block size 4.00" x 4.00", make the snap points 16 x 16, and the graph paper divisions 4 x 4. Another option is to use a separate block for the design in the corners.

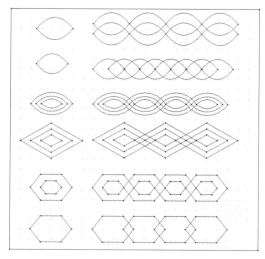

Geometric Border Variations

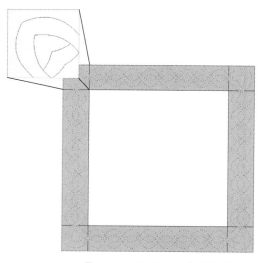

Try to create this border block

Drawing Thin Lines and Curves as Closed Shapes

Color block on page 72

Examples of thin lines as closed shapes

Step 3
Bezier Tool

Step 4
All Tools ON

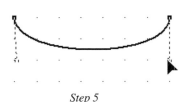

Step 5

Step 6
Select Tool

How thin can you make a shape in PatchDraw? This exercise is not a particular block, but I will show you how you can create closed shapes in PatchDraw that look as if they were one line or curve. Use this thin line technique for things like cat whiskers, flower stamens or lines to represent stitching patterns.

This exercise might seem sort of trivial, but it's necessary to learn this thin line technique to graduate to drawing designs for Sashiko in the next exercise.

1   On the BLOCK menu, point to New Block, click PatchDraw.

2   Also on the BLOCK menu, click Drawing Board Setup and enter these values:

General Tab
Snap to Grid Points
    Horizontal = 24   Vertical = 24
Block Size
    Horizontal = 6   Vertical = 6
Graph Paper Tab
Number of Divisions
    Horizontal = 2   Vertical = 2
Options
    Style = Graph paper lines

3   Click on the Bezier tool.

4   Click to turn Snap to Grid, Snap to Node, Auto Align Similar Lines and Snap Patch to Grid ON. Snap to Node and Auto Align Similar lines are on by default, but note that all tools are ON.

5   Draw a curve anywhere on the block that resembles a smile. The end nodes will snap to the nearest grid point where you begin and end the curve. Make any adjustments with the Bezier Edit tool before moving on to the next step.

6   Click on the Select tool.

2

7   Click on the curve to select it.

8   Click on the Copy button. (CTRL+C)

9   Click on the Paste button. (CTRL+V)

10   The copied curve will already be selected, but if it is not, click on it to select it.

11   Move the new curve *directly over* the first one and release the mouse. The new curve should snap right into place exactly over the first one and will look like one line.

12   Click on the Bezier Edit tool. Without clicking, point at one the nodes. You will see one of the tooltip messages: "Initial node in open curve with 1 arcs" or "Final node in open curve with 1 arcs."

13   Now click on one of the end nodes and the Auto-join feature of PatchDraw will automatically join the nodes. You won't see much happen except for a slight jump on the screen. After you have done this, point without clicking again and read the tooltip message. It should now say, "Middle corner node in open curve with 2 arcs."

14   Repeat Step 13 with the second node. The tooltip message for both nodes should now say, "Middle corner node in closed curve with 2 arcs."

15   Click on the Save in Sketchbook button to save your block.

Now you have a smile that looks like one line, but it is actually a closed shape made with two curves! Let's play with this smile a little and see what happens.

16   Still using the Bezier Edit tool, click on the curve so that you can see the handles.

Step 8
Copy Button

Step 9
Paste Button

Step 12
Bezier Edit Tool

Initial node in open curve with 1 arcs.

Step 12

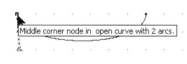

Middle corner node in open curve with 2 arcs.

Step 13

Step 15
Save in Sketchbook

2

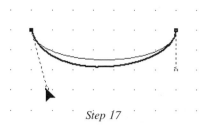

Step 17

Step 18
Line Tool

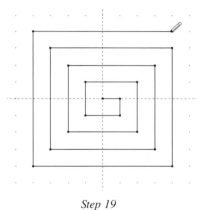

Step 19

Step 20
Select Tool

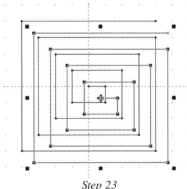

Step 23
Paste a copy of the line shape

17 Grab one of the handles (which are actually two handles, only they are lined up exactly and look like one handle) and drag it downward. As you do this you will see your smile open up. If you like, you can save this block in the Sketchbook.

Let's try one with straight lines now. We're going to draw a square maze design. Use the same block or place a new PatchDraw block on the Drawing Board. As in the first part of this exercise, make sure that Snap to Grid, Snap to Node, Auto Align Similar Lines and Snap Patch to Grid are turned ON.

18 Click on the Line tool.

19 Beginning at any grid point and drawing in a clockwise direction, draw a horizontal line 1/4" long. Release the mouse, change direction and draw a vertical line 1/4" long, creating a right angled shape. Release the mouse, change direction and draw a horizontal line 1/2" long. Change direction again and draw a vertical line 1/2" long. Continue in this manner, making sure you extend the line 1/4" beyond the previous round, until you have a maze design that is about 2.00" square.

20 Click on the Select tool.

21 Click on the line shape to select it.

22 Click on the Copy button.

23 Click on the Paste button.

2

24 With the copied line shape selected, drag it so it is placed exactly over the first one.

25 Click on the Bezier Edit tool.

26 Click on the end nodes. PatchDraw's auto-join feature will automatically join them.

27 Click on the Save in Sketchbook button to save your block.

As with the curved line we drew before, when you click on the node, the Auto-join feature will automatically join the nodes. Since straight lines do not have handles, you will need to check the tooltip message to see if your thin line shape is closed.

Experiment and try other thin line shapes like leaf veins, spirals or some of your own designs. When you get the hang of this thin line technique you will begin to see more uses!

If you want to make a spiral design, first draw a maze-like shape as in step 19. Next, use the Edit pop-up box to convert the straight lines to curves. Adjust the handles to round out the shape. Once you have your spiral, copy and paste it. Place the copied spiral over the first and then join the end nodes.

Step 25
Bezier Edit Tool

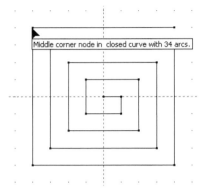

Middle corner node in closed curve with 34 arcs.

Check the tooltip message to see
if your shape is closed

Try variations such as leaf veins and spirals

116

Drawing Sashiko Designs in PatchDraw

Step 3
Select Tool

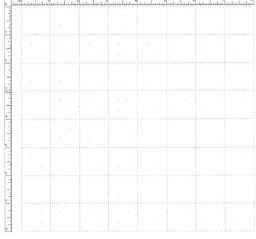

Step 4 – No Block Outline

Step 5
All Tools ON

Snap to Grid
Snap to Node
Auto Align Similar Lines
Snap Patch to Grid

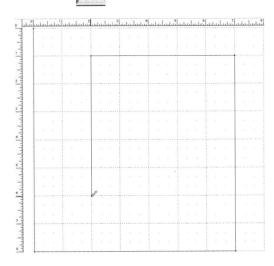

Sashiko is the traditional Japanese art of embroidering geometric designs with running stitches. Whether we stitch these designs in the classic style or use them for quilting, we can create them with PatchDraw.

We'll start with one of the most popular designs called Inazuma, which represents lightning. This design is similar to the square maze we drew in the last exercise, except that in Inazuma there is an exit to the maze and we will draw it as a full-size block. When the blocks are set side by side, they make a continuous design.

1   On the BLOCK menu, point to New Block, click PatchDraw.

2   Also on the BLOCK menu, click Drawing Board Setup and enter these values:

General Tab
Snap to Grid Points
   Horizontal = 24   Vertical = 24
Block Size
   Horizontal = 8   Vertical = 8
Graph Paper Tab
Number of Divisions
   Horizontal = 8   Vertical = 8
Options
   Style = Graph paper lines

3   Click on the Select tool.

4   We won't need the block outline, so let's remove it first. Click on the block outline to select it, then press your keyboard DELETE key.

5   On the Drawing toolbar, make sure that Snap to Grid, Snap to Node, Auto Align Similar Lines and Snap Patch to Grid are all ON.

6   Click on the Line tool.

2

⟍**Tip** ─────────────────────────────

- **This design is drawn as one continuous line. Release the mouse quickly and continue to draw from the same node when you change direction.**

2

7 Starting at the upper-left corner, draw a vertical line from top to bottom. Release the mouse quickly, change direction and draw a horizontal line from left to right across the block, releasing the mouse and changing direction at 7.00". Next draw a vertical line and change direction when you get to 1.00" from the top of the block. Draw a horizontal line and change direction at 2.00". Continue drawing and changing direction until you reach the center of the block as shown in the illustration.

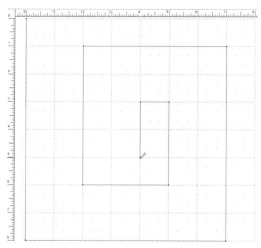

Step 7

8 Once you reach the center, draw a 1.00" horizontal line from right to left. Draw from the inside back to the outside of the block in the same manner, following the graph paper lines. End the drawing at the bottom-right corner as shown in the illustration.

9 Click on EDIT on the top menu bar. Click Select All (CTRL + A).

10 Click on the Copy button (CTRL + C).

11 Click on the Paste button (CTRL + V).

12 Drag the copied shape directly over the original and let it snap into place. It will look like one line.

13 Click on the Bezier Edit tool.

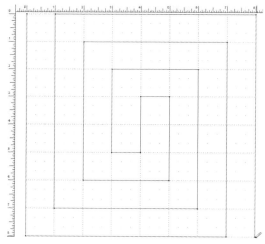

Step 8

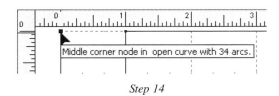

Step 14

Middle corner node in closed curve with 34 arcs.

Step 15

Step 16
Save in Sketchbook

Traditional Sashiko Quilt

14 Point to the end node in the upper-left corner and click on it to join the node to the one underneath. You will not see anything happen, except perhaps a little jump on the screen. If you point to the node without clicking you will see the tooltip message "Middle corner node in open curve with 34 arcs."

15 Point to the second end node in the lower-right corner. When the nodes are joined, the tooltip message will read, "Middle corner node in closed curve with 34 arcs."

16 Click on Save in Sketchbook to save your Inazuma design.

2

⟍ Tip

- **You will not be able to color this block! These thin line designs are used to represent stitching only. However, if you set this design on Layer 2 or 3 of the quilt worktable, you can change the color of the line with the Thread tool.**

To make a traditional Sashiko quilt, set up a horizontal quilt layout with one block (1 x 1). Use the Plain Block tool and fill the space with solid dark blue. When you place the Inazuma blocks on Layer 3, the white stitches will stand out. Use copy and paste on the quilt worktable to make copies of your new block if desired. Experiment with rotations and flipping and see what happens. If you like sashiko, check your local library or quilt shop for a book with more designs.

⟍ Tip

- **Copy and paste your designs on the drawing board until the block is filled as much as possible without going beyond the block outline. Keep Auto Align Similar Lines and Snap Patch to Grid ON, to make your shapes snap evenly.**

- **Many repeat designs can be set side by side on Layer 3 on the quilt worktable to cover a larger area. The snap feature on the quilt worktable will help you snap them together with ease.**

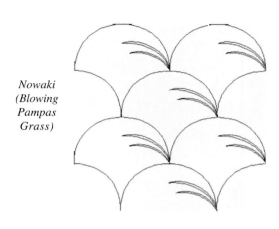

*Nowaki
(Blowing
Pampas
Grass)*

Tip

• **Most sashiko designs can also be used for continuous-line quilting designs. Print out the designs and use colored pencils or markers to trace the pattern.**

Here are three other traditional sashiko designs for you to try. The one with arcs and blades of grass was created with the thin line technique so that the sides and bottom could be left open. The other two were drawn as regular closed shapes and then cloned or resized in PatchDraw. All three were drawn with the Snap to Grid points set at 24 x 24. All the Advanced Drawing tools were turned ON, as in the exercise.

Inazuma Border and Juji Center

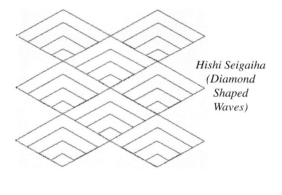

*Hishi Seigaiha
(Diamond
Shaped
Waves)*

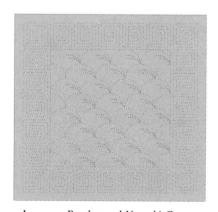

Inazuma Border and Nowaki Center

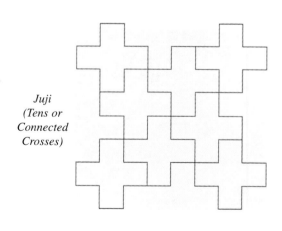

*Juji
(Tens or
Connected
Crosses)*

Chapter 3 Color Illustrations

Dresden Plate
Page 135

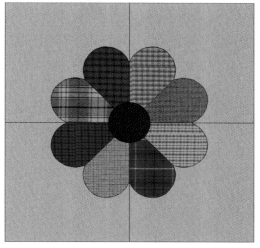

8-Petal Dresden Plate
Page 135

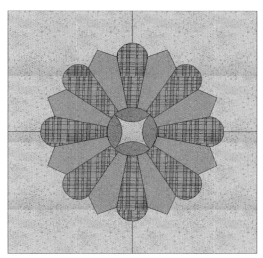

Fancy Dresden Plate
Page 135

Georgetown Circle
Page 145

3

3

Georgetown Circle Variation
Page 145

Mariner's Compass
Page 150

Mariner's Compass Variation
Page 150

Mariner's Compass Variation
Page 150

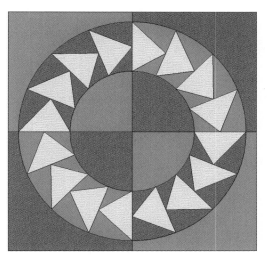

Circle of Geese
Page 154

Odd Angled Star
Page 159

Odd Angled Star Variation
Page 159

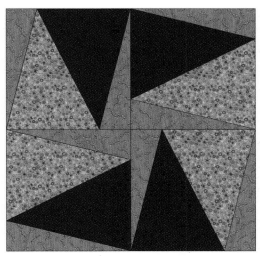

Odd Angled Star Variation
Page 159

3

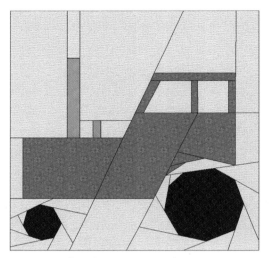

Complex Paper Pieced Pattern
Page 162

Rolling Stone
Page 167

Rolling Stone Variation
Page 167

Rolling Stone Variation
Page 167

More Advanced Drawing

Chapter 3

Chapter 3 Overview

If you worked through most of the exercises in the previous chapter, you discovered that the Advanced Drawing Features open a whole new world of possibilities in designing blocks. In this chapter, we'll work almost entirely in EasyDraw™ and concentrate on using nodes. We won't use the Advanced Drawing Features in every exercise, but only as we need them.

I view many of the blocks in this chapter as "possibility blocks". Work through the exercises to learn the process, and then use your new skills to create your own one-of-a-kind blocks. We'll learn to use nodes in a variety of ways to accomplish the task at hand. There will be lots of practice playing "connect the dots"! We'll play a little more with eight-point star designs and even try our hand at complex paper piecing designs. Oh yes, and before I forget… we will begin with a little detour and learn how to use EQ5 block metafiles in Microsoft Word™.

3

Using EQ5 Metafiles in Microsoft Word™

While this exercise is not about *drawing* a block, it is definitely related to the blocks and the drawing board in EQ5. If you teach quilting classes and like to make great looking handouts, or if you are in charge of the newsletter for your quilt guild, EQ5's metafile feature is the ticket for getting your quilt block images into your document.

This is not meant to be a tutorial on how to use Microsoft Word™, but is intended to show you how to use EQ5's Export Metafile feature effectively. There is a wealth of information interspersed among the steps, so do your homework and learn just some of the possibilities with this feature!

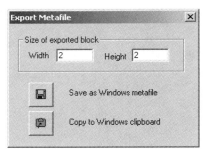

Step 2
Export Metafile Button

Steps 3 – 4

⚲ Tip ─────────────

• **This exercise was written using Microsoft Word™ 2000 and 2002. Microsoft Word™ 97 works much the same way, except the Format Picture dialog and tabs are different. Word™ 97 has two separate tabs called Position and Wrapping, whereas newer versions of Word™ group these options under one tab, Layout.**

1 Open an EQ5 project file of your choice that contains a block you would like to illustrate in your document. I will use the Sawtooth Star block. Click on View Sketchbook and click on the block to select it. Then, click on Edit to place the block on the drawing board.

⚲ Tip ─────────────

• **You can only export metafiles of blocks, not quilts. They must be exported from the block worktable.**

2 Click on the Export Metafile button. This will bring up the Export Metafile box.

3 In the Export Metafile box, type in the size. In this example I will use 2.00" x 2.00".

4 Click on the button that says, Save as Windows metafile.

Steps 5 – 7

Microsoft
Word

Step 8
Microsoft Word™ icon

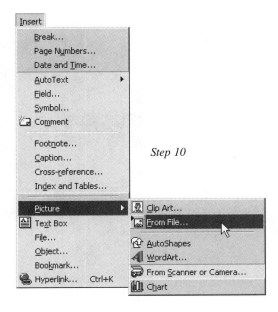

Step 10

5 Navigate to where you want to save the file by clicking the down arrow beside Save in. I store my metafiles in a subfolder I created called Metafiles in the main My EQ5 folder where projects and bitmaps are stored in separate subfolders.

6 Name the metafile by typing it in the box beside File name. You do not need to change Save as type, since it will say Enhanced Metafiles by default.

7 Click on Save. The file will be saved with the extension **.emf**.

8 Open a document in Microsoft Word™ in which you would like to add the block from EQ5. *I recommend that you just use a practice document for now, especially if you have not used metafiles before. Have fun with this exercise and play to learn!*

Tip

• **Instead of saving the metafile, you will find it much faster if you use the Copy to Windows Clipboard button when you export your metafile. You can have both EQ5 and Microsoft Word™ open simultaneously so that switching from one program to the other is as close as a click on your Windows taskbar.**

9 In your Microsoft Word™ document, click near the area where you would like to place the block. Once you have the metafile inserted and make a few changes, you will be able to move it around on the page.

10 In Microsoft Word™, on the Insert Menu, point to Picture and then click From File.

11 In the Insert Picture box, navigate to the folder where you saved the EQ5 metafile.

3

12 Select the file or type the name in the box beside File name. You should not need to change Files of type. By default, the Files of type will include a list of common types of graphics along with the **.emf** extension. If you do not see it in the list, click the down arrow and choose it.

13 Click on Insert. The metafile should now be inserted into your document.

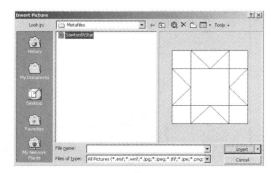

Step 12

When a block from EQ5 is converted to a metafile, it will be a line drawing without color. It is magically transformed into a block where all the patches are separate closed shapes.

The block pieces are ungrouped automatically and can be individually manipulated. In a Word™ document, the metafile block is a drawing object, and it can be treated as any other line drawing using any of the features on Word™'s Drawing toolbar. You will learn more about that later!

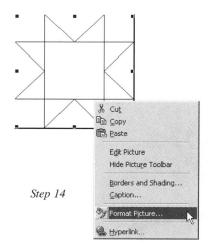

Step 14

By default, when you insert an object into Word™, it will be *in line* with the text. What that means is that images are affected just as if they were text, and can only be moved as if they were text. There are options in Word™ to change how an image is inserted, but if you would like to do this, please do that on your own. It will not be covered in this book. Now, let's get back to work!

The first thing I do after inserting the block picture is to change the image so that it floats above the text and then I can have the freedom to move it on the page where I like. Think of the document as having two layers – one for text and one for graphics. If the image remains on the text layer, you will be very limited in how you can move it.

14 Right-click on the image, and in the context menu choose Format Picture (also accessible via the main FORMAT menu).

3

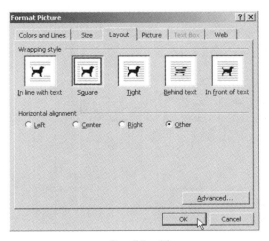

Step 15 – 16

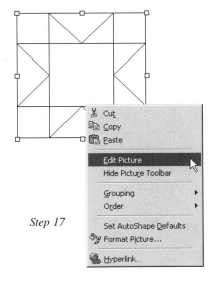

Step 17

15 In the Format Picture box, click on the Layout tab.

16 On the Layout tab, you will see several different word wrapping styles. Click on the one that says Square and then click OK. (In Word 97™, click on the Position tab and *check* the box beside Float over text and then on the Wrapping tab, choose Square.)

17 Right-click on the block graphic again and choose Edit Picture. If you are asked if you want to convert it to a Microsoft Office™ drawing object, say yes.

You will need to do some experimenting (a.k.a. playing) with your particular version of Word™ to see what happens when you complete Step 17, but here are a few helpful hints.

In Word™ 97 and Word™ 2000, when you edit a picture, the screen will automatically zoom in on the picture for you to edit. In Word™ 2002, it does not zoom in on the picture, but you work on the drawing "as is."

In all versions, the block should now be surrounded by a tight-fitting box. A floating toolbar will also appear. (If you do not see the floating toolbar, go to the VIEW menu, point to Toolbars and click on Edit Picture to check it.) The purpose of the box is to keep your image parts together so that they can be moved as a unit. It also makes word wrapping look neater.

In Word™ 97 and Word™ 2000 this tight-fitting box is a fixed shape until you click on Resize to Fit Image on the floating toolbar that appears when you are editing a picture. In Word™ 2002, this box is called the "Drawing Canvas" and is similar to a selection box that can be resized and moved manually. The Drawing Canvas toolbar appears when it is selected.

3

With that information behind us, editing the block is the easy part! Let's work through a simple block piecing diagram so that we can learn some of the uses for our exported metafile. I will use the Sawtooth Star in this example.

18   First, make the Drawing Toolbar in Word™ visible, if it is not already. On the VIEW menu, point to Toolbars and then click on Drawing to check it.

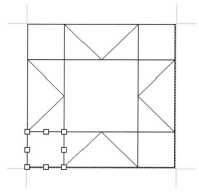

Each patch is a separate object in Microsoft Word™

Remember, the block metafile we exported from EQ5 is now made up of separate shapes. When you are in the "edit picture" mode, the patches of the block are already ungrouped. You can click on each one separately or hold down the SHIFT key to multiple select. Let's take our block apart to see how this works.

Notice that when you hold the cursor over the block, it changes to a pointer and crossed arrows indicating that you can select parts of your drawing.

In Word 97™ and 2000, you can move block parts without resizing the box frame around them. After you have finished editing, you must resize it to fit around the shapes. On the Edit picture toolbar, click on Resize to fit image.

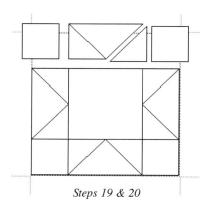

Steps 19 & 20

In Word 2002™, you need to expand the Drawing Canvas first so that everything stays on the canvas. The Drawing Canvas can be resized by grabbing the corner or sides, or by clicking on Expand on the floating toolbar. When you are finished editing your block, click on Fit to make the canvas fit snug again.

19   Click on the top-left corner square of the block and drag it to the left slightly. Then do the same for the square on the top-right. You can also use the arrow keys on your keyboard to move the shapes in smaller increments.

3

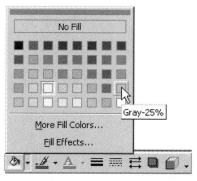

Step 22

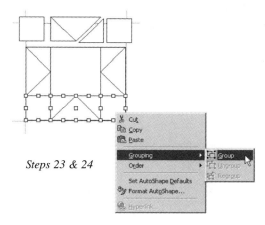

Steps 23 & 24

20 Select one of the side triangles of the star point unit and move it slightly away from the center triangle.

21 Now let's color the block in grayscale so that it will make nice photocopies. Holding down the SHIFT key, select all the star point triangles. You only need to click in the center of the shapes to select them.

22 Once you have the shapes selected, click on the down arrow on the Drawing toolbar beside the Fill Color tool. Select one of the grays to fill your shapes with color.

23 Let's group the bottom parts of the block so that they move as a unit. Holding down the SHIFT key, select all the shapes you want to group, then right-click to open the context menu.

24 On the context menu, point to Grouping and then click on Group. Now you can move this unit together when you click on any part of it. Repeat with any of the other shapes you want to group.

Those are the basics of using an EQ5 metafile in Word™. Please take the time to experiment. Insert several metafiles from EQ5 into a Word™ document and just play! I cannot possibly cover everything in a book on block drawing, but here are a few other helpful hints for handouts, newsletters, pattern directions, and more.

3

Tip

- If you want to add text to your block, use the Text Box tool or Word Art™. Text boxes are essentially a box that you can type in and you have the paragraph formatting available to use. The text box outline can be removed if needed. Word Art™ shapes have all the characteristics of drawings and are a quick way to add just one letter to a block diagram.

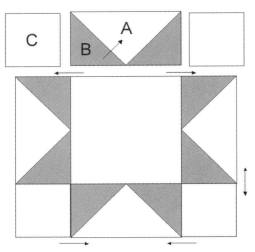

You can add text labels and arrows to make great looking class handouts.

Tip

- Use the Line tools to draw dashed lines to indicate stitching lines. You can change the thickness and style of lines as needed.

- Use the Arrow tools to draw small arrows to indicate pressing direction. You can even change the style of the arrowhead if you like.

- Copy and paste parts of the block to use for cutting charts and sub-unit piecing.

- Image can be resized proportionally by grabbing the corner handles. You can also resize to an exact size in the Format Picture box on the size tab.

- Don't forget appliqué blocks! You can also export appliqué blocks as metafiles – with or without the block outline.

- There are really cool options for fill effects in Word™. Click on the down arrow beside the Fill Color tool and click on Fill Effects. On the Patterns tab, you can use two-color patterns to fill your shapes. These are not real fancy, but they copy very well if you are making handouts. On the Texture tab, you can use tiled images...like fabric bitmaps exported from EQ5 or STASH!

- On the Drawing toolbar in Word™, there are a lot more options to explore if you click on where it says Draw... helpful things like aligning shapes, flipping, rotating, ordering the layers and even snap to grid. In Word 2000™ and Word 2002™, you can even make the grid visible on the page if you like. You will also find Snap to Object. This is *extremely* helpful if you need to put parts of your block back together again.

- Are those block pictures not staying on the document page where you thought you placed them? By default, images are anchored to the text where they were *inserted* and they will move with that. This can be a plus, but if you have made a lot of corrections and additions in your document, your images will go all over the place. You can undo this by un-checking the "Move object with text" option. You will find this by clicking on the Layout tab of the Format Picture dialog and clicking on the Advanced button. You must do each image separately.

Please take time to play and explore the possibilities of metafiles in Word™. Metafiles are a wonderful feature that the makers of EQ5 have given us and I'm sure you'll discover even more cool ways to use them!

Drawing a Traditional Dresden Plate Block

Color blocks on page 121

Dresden Plate Block

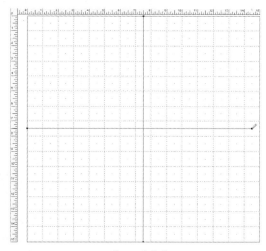

Steps 4 & 5

The Dresden Plate block can be made with any number of petals or blades, but the traditional Dresden Plate design has sixteen blades and a 3.00" center circle. In drawing this block, you'll see how deleting lines can be part of the process.

1   On the BLOCK menu, point to New Block, click EasyDraw™. Turn Snap to Grid ON, Snap to Node ON, Snap to Drawing OFF.

2   Also on the BLOCK menu, click Drawing Board Setup and enter these values:

General Tab
Snap to Grid Points
    Horizontal = 60   Vertical = 60
Block Size
    Horizontal = 15   Vertical = 15
Graph Paper Tab
Number of Divisions
    Horizontal = 15   Vertical = 15
Options
    Style = Graph paper lines

Since we are working on a 15.00" block, we need to draw guidelines to help us find the center of the block.

3   Click on the Line tool.

4   Draw a vertical line from top to bottom at 7.50" from the left.

5   Draw a horizontal line across the block at 7.50" from the top.

6   Click on the Select tool.

7   Right-click on the drawing board. Click on Convert to Guides.

8   Click on the Arc tool.

3

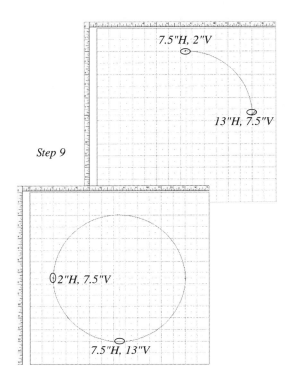

Step 9

Tip

- **To make an arc flip in the opposite direction, press the Spacebar on your keyboard before releasing the mouse button.**

9 Point your mouse at the top center, 2.00" down from the block outline. You're going to start from this point to draw the first of four arcs which will form a circle. To draw an arc, drag the mouse and release it when you reach the start point of the next arc at 2.00" in from the right side of the block outline on the horizontal center line. Going in a clockwise direction, draw three more arcs to complete the circle.

10 Measuring from the block outline, draw two more circles (four arcs each), going from larger to smaller, at 2 3/4" and 6" inside the first one.

Remember that even though you cannot see them, there are four grid points per inch. This is equivalent to a point every 1/4" in a 15" block.

Tip

- **Once the circles are drawn, you can turn off the graph paper lines. Click on the Hide/Show Graph Paper lines button to easily turn them off and on.**

11 Click on the Line tool.

12 Draw four straight anchor lines from each of the connecting nodes on the largest circle to the block outline. This is necessary since we are drawing this as a pieced block.

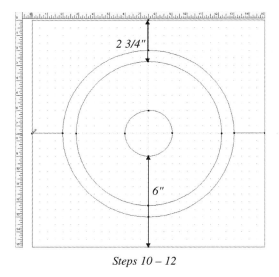

Steps 10 – 12

Step 15

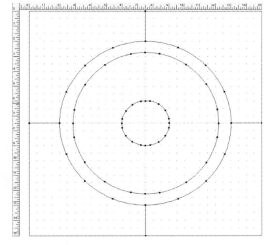

Step 21

13 Click on the Save in Sketchbook button to save the block at this stage.

14 Click on the small black square in the corner of the Edit tool to open the Edit Arc box.

15 On the Edit Arc box, change the number beside Partition to 4, and then change the number beside Stagger to 4.

16 Click on one of the arcs of the *largest* circle to select it.

17 On the Edit Arc box, click on Partition to partition this arc into four segments. Repeat this partitioning with the remaining three arcs of the outer circle.

18 Click on one of the arcs of the *second largest* circle to select it.

19 On the Edit Arc box, click on Stagger. Repeat with the remaining three arcs of this circle.

20 Click on one of the arcs of the *smallest* circle to select it.

21 On the Edit Arc box, click on Stagger. Repeat with the remaining three arcs of this circle.

3

22 Click on the Line tool.

23 Turn OFF Snap to Grid. Turning this off will make it easier for the lines to snap to the nodes and not the grid points.

24 Draw lines to connect the nodes between the *smallest* circle and the *second largest* circle to form the blades of the Dresden Plate, ignoring the nodes where the arcs connect.

25 To create the points on top of the blades, draw lines in a zigzag manner going back and forth between the nodes of the outer circles.

At this design stage, you can see the Dresden Plate. Now we need to delete the lines not needed in the block. You may want to save the block to the Sketchbook again before proceeding to the next step.

Step 23
Snap to Grid OFF

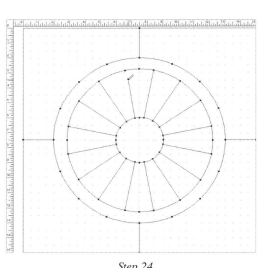

Step 24

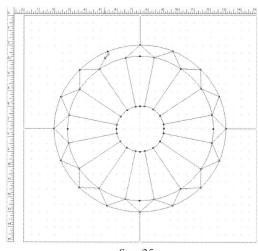

Step 25

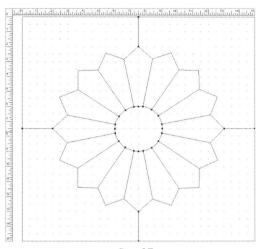

Step 27

26 Click on the Select tool.

27 Delete all the arc segments of the two outer circles. You can delete lines and arcs one at a time by clicking a line then pressing the keyboard DELETE key. Or, you can hold down the SHIFT key and click on arc after arc until all are selected. When you are finished deleting the arcs, the block is complete.

28 Click on the Save in Sketchbook button to save your block.

Tip

• **If you reverse the Partition and Stagger on the circles, the center lines of the block will be between the blades instead of in the center of the blades. See the Dresden Plate blocks in the EQ5 Block Library under Classic Pieced for examples.**

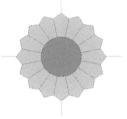

Completed Dresden Plate block

Try one with a larger center circle.

To make one with curved petals as opposed to pointed blades, use the Arc tool and draw two arcs on top of each section. Or, alternate between petals and blades.

3

Converting an EasyDraw™ Block into a Motif

If you have ever sewn a Dresden Plate block, you know that it's part pieced and part appliqué. To create accurate templates, I recommend drawing the block in EasyDraw™. However, if you want to make your Dresden Plate a free floating motif, you can do this easily using an Overlaid block and WreathMaker.

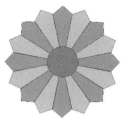

Motif

Try this exercise first with the Dresden Plate block created in the previous exercise. Once you learn the technique, you will be able to apply the knowledge to any block you choose.

1 Click on the View Sketchbook button and select the Dresden Plate block. Click Edit to place the block on the EasyDraw™ worktable.

Remember that the Drawing Board Setup is the same as in the previous section. (See page 135 for values.)

✎ Tip

• **To make the nodes visible when you place a block on the worktable to edit, use the Select tool and click twice slowly on any line of the drawing. Do not double-click, but click on the line once to select it and then click on the same line again. If you accidentally move the line, use CTRL+Z immediately to undo it.**

2 On the EDIT menu, click Select All (or use CTRL+A).

3 Click on the Copy button (or use CTRL+C).

4 On the BLOCK, menu point to New Block, click Overlaid. By default, you will be on the Pieced layer when working on a new Overlaid block.

5 Click on the Paste button (or use CTRL+V) to place the Dresden Plate on the Pieced layer. While the block is still selected, move it so that it snaps into place and the straight anchor lines are centered. The top center is 7 1/2" if you are using the 15" Dresden Plate from the previous exercise.

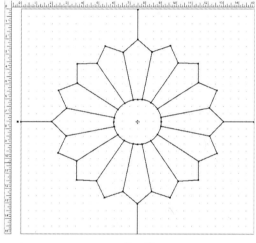

Step 2

Step 4

Step 6

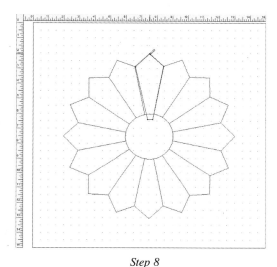
Step 8

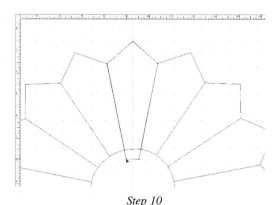
Step 10

6   Click on the Appliqué layer tab.

7   Click on the Line tool.

We only need to trace one blade of the Dresden Plate. However, we need to trace the top center blade since we need an upright shape to use for Wreathmaker.

8   Trace *only* the top blade of the Dresden Plate. Click on the Zoom tool and zoom-in on the top blade so that you can make your adjustments as neat as possible.

I find it easier to trace in a clockwise direction beginning at the top point of the blade. I end back at the same node where I began, thus ensuring that I get a closed patch. When you trace around the narrow end of the blade, extend the lines so that they are within the center circle (just like actual appliqué). Don't worry if your lines are not perfectly aligned as you trace, we can fine tune them once we get a closed shape.

9   Click on the Edit Bezier tool.

10   Click on the nodes, and adjust them so that they are aligned with the nodes of the Pieced layer image. We only need to move the *nodes* around since we are working with straight lines.

You can actually get a near perfect tracing if you zoom-in really close to do your final tweaking of the appliqué patch. Notice that when you are adjusting the lines of the appliqué shape and they line up with those of the pieced layer image, they seem to disappear. Once you release the mouse button they will reappear. This may or may not happen, depending on your monitor's screen resolution, but generally you can see some change in the lines when they are moved over the ones on the Pieced layer image.

3

11 Once you are satisfied with the appliqué patch, click on the Save in Sketchbook button to save the block at this stage.

12 Click on the Select tool.

13 Click on the patch to select it.

14 Right-click, then click WreathMaker on the context menu.

15 Set the WreathMaker values as follows:

Number of Clusters 16
Cluster Spacing 36%
Resize Cluster 100%

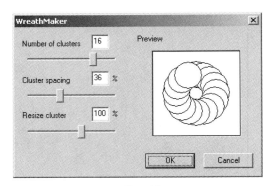

Step 15

Our goal is to create a wreath with blade patches touching but not overlapping. You may need to change the percentage for Cluster Spacing slightly, but the Number of Clusters and Cluster Size should not be changed. If there are small uneven gaps, it may be due to the original patch and not WreathMaker. Small fluctuations really won't matter since this motif is for design purposes, not necessarily for a pattern. For precise templates, use the EasyDraw™ Dresden Plate.

Step 16

When you are satisfied with your wreath, save the block in the Sketchbook, then continue to the next step.

16 Make sure you are on the Appliqué layer of the Overlaid block, then click on the Select tool.

3

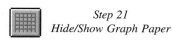

Step 21
Hide/Show Graph Paper

Step 23
Circle Shape

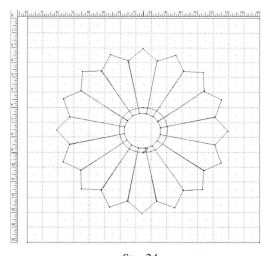

Step 24

17 On the EDIT menu, click Select All (or CTRL+A).

18 Click on Copy (or CTRL+C).

19 On the BLOCK menu, point to New Block, click PatchDraw.

20 Click on Paste (or CTRL+V) to paste the Dresden Plate on the new block. If needed, move the wreath while it is still selected so that it is centered in the block, then click off the wreath to deselect it.

21 Making the circle patch in the center is easy in PatchDraw. If you do not have the graph paper lines showing, click on the Hide/Show Graph Paper tool to make them visible.

22 Turn ON Snap to Grid and Snap Patch to Grid. These two features will help you draw a near perfect circle with more precise placement.

23 Click on the small black triangle to open the Simple Oval tool fly-out and choose the circle shape.

24 Look at the graph paper lines and locate the three inch grid in the center of the block. Point the cursor near the top vertical center of this three inch grid (at 6.00") and drag the mouse to the bottom center (at 9.00").

3

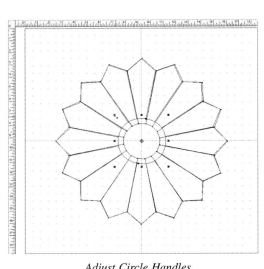

- **The Simple Oval circle generally results in a circle that is a little too wide. Usually this is not a problem, but for our Dresden Plate we want a nice round center. Using the Select tool, select the drawn circle and adjust the side nodes so that the circle's width is within this three inch graph paper line grid.**

25 To make your Dresden Plate a free-floating motif, there is one more step. Use the Select tool and click on the block outline to select it. Then press the DELETE key on your keyboard to delete the square block outline.

26 Click on the Save in Sketchbook button.

Now that you have converted your Dresden Plate to an appliqué motif, you can use it on Layer 2 of a quilt layout like any appliqué.

Adjust Circle Handles

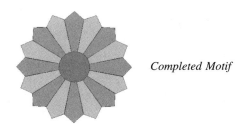

Completed Motif

3

Drawing a Georgetown Circle

Color blocks on pages 121 – 122

Georgetown Circle

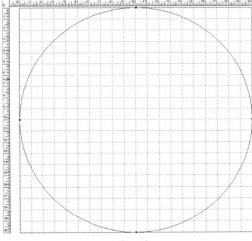

Step 4

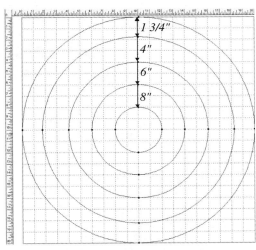

Step 5

There are lots of design possibilities with arcs in EQ5 when you partition and stagger nodes. Practice your connect-the-dot skills with the nodes on this block, then try some of the variations following this lesson.

1   On the BLOCK menu, point to New Block, click EasyDraw™. Turn Snap to Grid ON, Snap to Node ON, Snap to Drawing OFF.

2   Also on the BLOCK menu, click Drawing Board Setup and enter these values:

General Tab
Snap to Grid Points
    Horizontal = 80   Vertical = 80
Block Size
    Horizontal = 20   Vertical = 20
Graph Paper Tab
Number of Divisions
    Horizontal = 20   Vertical = 20
Options
    Style = Graph paper lines

3   Click on the Arc tool.

4   Starting at the top center, draw four arcs to make a complete circle that fills the block.

5   Measuring in from the block outline, going from the larger to the smaller, draw four more circles (four arcs each) at 1 3/4", 4", 6" and 8" inside the first one.

Think of a clock. I draw my circles clockwise, beginning at 12 o'clock (top center). As you draw the circles, note the distance from the previous circle as you park each arc at 3 o'clock, 6 o'clock and 9 o'clock. All end nodes of the arcs will fall on a graph paper intersection except the second largest circle. There are four snap points per graph paper square, so finding 1 3/4" will be easy.

3

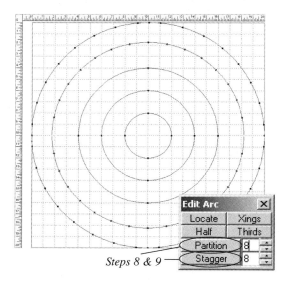

Tip

- Once the circles are drawn, you can click on the Hide/Show Graph Paper tool to turn the graph paper lines off, but you don't have to.

6 Click on the small black square in the corner of the Edit tool to open the Edit Arc box.

7 On the Edit Arc box, change the numbers beside Partition and Stagger to 8.

8 Click on each of the four outside arcs that make up the largest circle one at a time, and then click on Stagger.

Tip

- Dragging the Edit Arc box onto the drawing board makes it easier to do the Partition and Stagger process. Point to the top frame of the Edit Arc box and hold down the left mouse button. Drag it to the location you want it.

9 Click on each of the four arcs that make up the second largest circle, then click on Partition.

10 On the Edit Arc box, change the number beside Partition to 4.

11 Click on each of the arcs that make up the two innermost circles and click on Partition again.

Now we have all the nodes established for the block. All we need to do is connect the dots!

12 Click on the Snap to Grid button to turn it OFF.

Steps 8 & 9

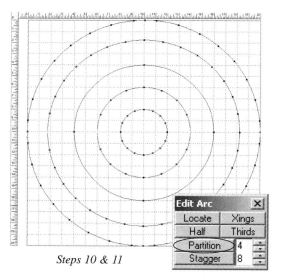

Steps 10 & 11

Step 12
Snap to Grid OFF

Step 13
Line Tool

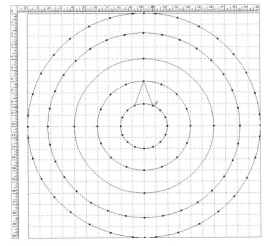

Steps 14 & 15

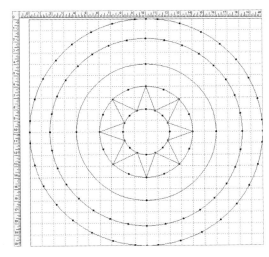

Step 15 completed

 Tip —————————————————

- **Whenever you are drawing a block similar to this one containing a lot of nodes to connect with lines, turn OFF Snap to Grid.**

- **As you draw the block, save it to the Sketchbook at different stages. This not only gives you a backup copy of the block, but allows you to edit them at different stages to make variations.**

13 Click on the Line tool.

Let's begin by drawing the larger star points around the center circle.

14 The first star point is pointing up at 12 o'clock. On the inner circle, begin at the node to the left of the top-center node. Draw a line to the top-center node at 12 o'clock on the next largest circle.

15 Starting at the same node where you left off, draw the second half of the star point ending on the opposite node to the right of center. Draw the remaining star points in this zigzag manner, skipping every other node around the circles, until you have eight identical star points around the center.

3

16 Draw lines extending from each of the central star points and every node in between, out to the nodes along the second largest circle. Skip every other node on the second largest circle.

Notice we did not need to partition the arcs of one of the circles. Nodes will be established along these arcs when the block is saved in the Sketchbook.

17 Now for the last round of this block. Draw the first line of the triangle point beginning at the top center node on the second largest circle and ending on the node to the right of the top center node on the largest circle. Again, work in a zigzag motion as you draw the remaining triangle points.

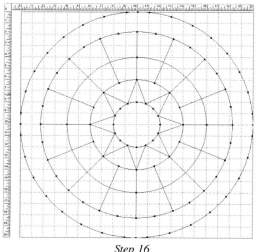

Step 16

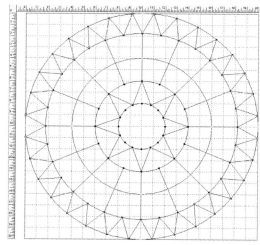

Step 17

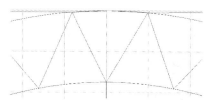

Use the Zoom tool to get a closer look.

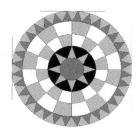

Completed Georgetown Circle

*Here are two variations using
the same circles and partitions.*

Tip
- Whenever you are drawing triangle points that fall along an arc near the block outline, be sure to zoom in to make *sure* that the lines are attached to the nodes along the arc and not the block outline.

18 Click on the Save to Sketchbook button to save your new block.

Tip
- You can make this block paper piecing friendly by adding a few lines which will divide the rounds of triangle points into quarters. When you go to print the foundation pattern, on the Sections tab, regroup the sections as needed to make paper piecing possible. Use those cool features in the Print Preview to move and delete sections then print out only what you need!

3

Drawing a Mariner's Compass Block

Color blocks on page 122

This exercise shows how to draw a traditional style Mariner's Compass block. There are so many possibilities with this block that the only rule is that it should have at least four points to indicate North, South, East, and West. Try this version first and learn how *deleting* lines is a major part of the design process.

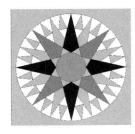

Mariner's Compass Block

1   On the BLOCK menu, point to New Block, click EasyDraw™. Turn Snap to Grid ON, Snap to Node ON, Snap to Drawing OFF.

2   Also on the BLOCK menu, click Drawing Board Setup and enter these values:

General Tab
Snap to Grid Points
    Horizontal = 48   Vertical = 48
Block Size
    Horizontal = 12   Vertical = 12
Graph Paper Tab
Number of Divisions
    Horizontal = 12   Vertical = 12
Options
    Style = Graph paper lines

3   Click on the Arc tool.

4   Starting at the top center and 1/2" in from the block outline, draw four arcs to make a circle.

5   Measuring in from the block outline, and going from the larger to the smaller, draw three more circles (four arcs each) at 2", 3", and 4 1/2" inside the first one. Once you have your circles drawn, you can turn off the graph paper lines.

6   Click on the Line tool.

7   Draw four short anchor lines from the center nodes to connect the arcs to the block outline.

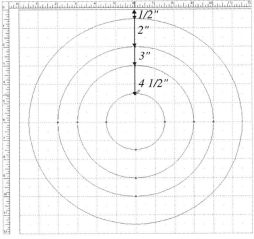

Steps 4 & 5

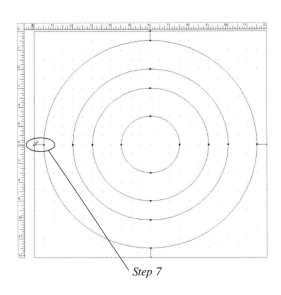

Step 7

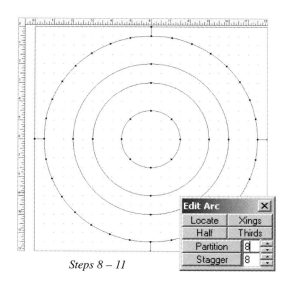

Steps 8 – 11

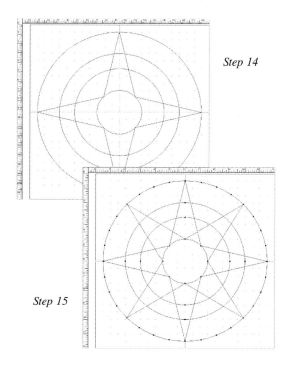

Step 14

Step 15

8 Click on the small black square in the corner of the Edit tool to open the Edit Arc box.

9 On the Edit Arc box, change the number beside Partition to 8.

10 Click on each of the arcs of the largest circle, then click on Partition on the Edit Arc box.

11 Next, click on each arc of the small center circle, then click on Half on the Edit Arc box.

12 Click on the Snap to Grid button to turn it OFF.

13 Click on the Line tool.

14 Skipping every other node on the inner circle, draw the four long compass points extending to the outer circle that represent North, South, East, and West, as shown.

15 Using the remaining nodes on the inner circle, draw four more long compass points to the outer circle, centering them between the first four, as shown.

3

16 Click on the Save in Sketchbook button. This will establish nodes for the next round of compass points. If you can't see the new nodes, click on the Refresh button to make them visible.

17 Drawing from the new nodes on the second smallest circle to the outer circle, draw eight compass points between each of the existing ones.

18 Click on Save in Sketchbook again.

19 Drawing from the new nodes established, draw sixteen compass points between each of the existing ones.

The compass design is complete now, but the block isn't finished until we delete some of the lines we used to create it.

Refresh Button

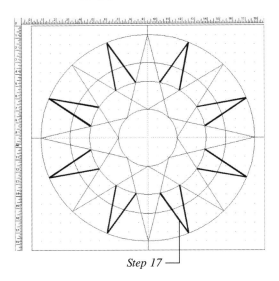

Step 17

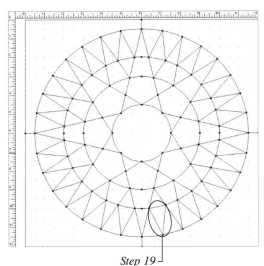

Step 19
Draw 16 of these small compass points

3

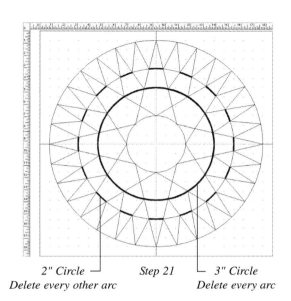

2" Circle — Step 21 └ 3" Circle
Delete every other arc *Delete every arc*

20 Click on the Select tool.

21 Holding down the SHIFT key, multiple-select all the arc lines of the 3" circle and press the DELETE key on your keyboard. Again, holding down the SHIFT key, select every *other* arc of the 2" circle, starting with the North point of the compass, and press the DELETE key on your keyboard. Click the Refresh button as needed to clean up what is left behind when you delete.

22 Click on the Save in Sketchbook button.

Completed Mariner's Compass Block

The oval compass is made by just changing the block size.

Here are a few variations. To foundation piece the compass points, delete all the remaining arcs within the design and replace them with straight lines.

3

Drawing a Circle of Geese Block

Color block on page 123

One of the basic shapes of quilting – the triangle – takes off in a new direction in this block!

1   On the BLOCK menu, point to New Block, click EasyDraw™. Turn Snap to Grid ON, Snap to Node ON, Snap to Drawing OFF.

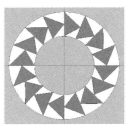

Circle of Geese Block

2   Also on the BLOCK menu, click Drawing Board Setup and enter these values:

General Tab
Snap to Grid Points
    Horizontal = 24   Vertical = 24
Block Size
    Horizontal = 6   Vertical = 6
Graph Paper Tab
Number of Divisions
    Horizontal = 6   Vertical = 6
Options
    Style = Graph paper lines

3   Click on the Line tool.

4   Draw a horizontal line from left to right across the block at 3.00" from the top and a vertical line from top to bottom at 3.00" from the left, creating a Four Patch block.

5   Click on the Arc tool.

We'll draw just one quarter of the geese circle, then use Clone and Rotate to complete the block.

6   Draw two arcs in the upper-left quadrant of the block. Drawing from right to left, draw the first arc beginning at the horizontal center of the block 1/4" from the top of the block and ending it at the vertical center 1/4" from the left side of the block. Draw the second arc, beginning at 1 1/2" from the top center and ending at 1 1/2" from the left center.

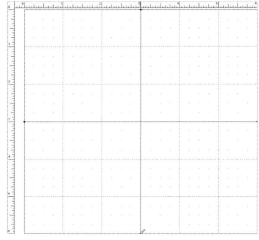

Step 4

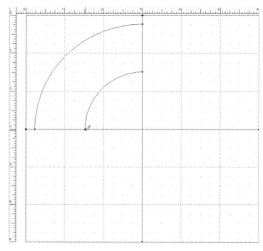

Step 6

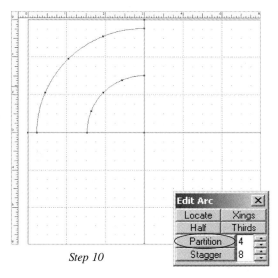

Step 10

Edit Arc ☒
Locate	Xings
Half	Thirds
Partition	4
Stagger	8

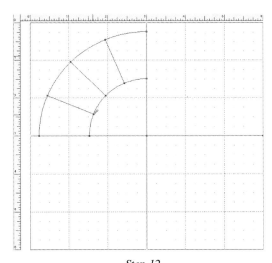

Step 12

7   Click on the Save in Sketchbook button to establish nodes where the arcs meet the center lines.

8   Click on the small black square in the corner of the Edit tool to open the Edit Arc box.

9   On the Edit Arc box, change the number beside Partition to 4.

10   Click on one of the arcs to select it, and then click on Partition. Repeat with the other arc so that both arcs are partitioned into 4 segments.

11   Click on the Line tool.

12   Drawing across from arc to arc, draw three straight lines to connect the three sets of nodes along the arcs.

13   Save the block in the Sketchbook to establish nodes. You will also have the block saved at this stage in case you want to try something different later.

Next, we need to add a node on the lines between the arcs so that we will have a center point to use when drawing the geese triangles.

14   Click on the Edit tool, then click on one of the straight lines we drew between the arcs, to select it.

3

15 Click on the small black square in the corner of the Edit tool to open the Edit Arc box, if it is not already open. Click on Half. This will add a node in the center of the line. Repeat with the remaining four straight lines, including the two segments that fall along the horizontal and vertical center lines. There are 5 lines total to which we need to add a node. You cannot multiple-select lines to segment, so you must select each one separately and then click on Half.

16 Click on the Line tool.

17 Turn OFF Snap to Grid.

18 Draw the two angled lines to make four geese triangles between the arcs as illustrated. You can have your geese flying clockwise or counterclockwise, that's up to you! Once you have them drawn, save the block in the Sketchbook.

19 Turn Snap to Grid back ON.

20 Click on the small black square in the corner of the Select tool to open the Symmetry box.

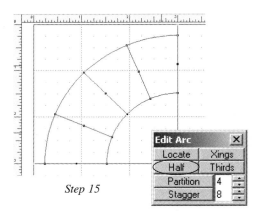

Step 15

Step 17
Snap to Grid

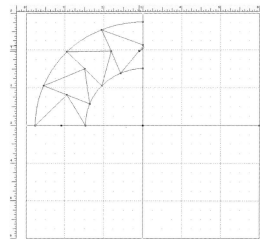

Step 18

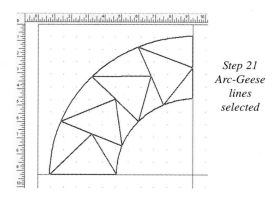

*Step 21
Arc-Geese
lines
selected*

21 Point to just above the top-left corner of your geese drawing and drag a selection box around the entire upper-left quadrant so that the arcs and geese are selected. This selects a little more than we need, so we need to de-select some lines. Hold down the SHIFT key on your keyboard and click on the parts of the horizontal and vertical center lines that are not within the arc. Another option would be to hold down the SHIFT key and click on all the lines of the arc-geese, but that takes a little longer to do.

22 On the Symmetry box, click on Clone and then click on Rot 90. Move the cloned section to the upper-right quadrant, aligning the nodes carefully and making *sure* it snaps into place when you release the mouse. *Keep the newest section selected* and then repeat Clone and Rot 90 two more times, moving each new section to its respective quadrant to complete the block.

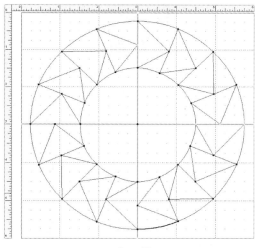

Step 22

3

23 Once all parts are snapped into place, you can save the final block in the Sketchbook.

Now that you know the process, try some of your own variations of this circular geese block. Try varying the width of the arcs and adding more geese if you like. You could even draw more than one circle of geese on one block.

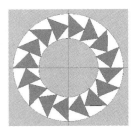

Completed Circle of Geese Block

Tip ─────────────────

• **Foundation piecing is the preferred method for sewing these geese arcs. The rest of the block construction would be similar to piecing a Drunkard's Path block. On the Section tab of the Print Foundation dialog, redefine the sections so that each arc of geese is one grouped unit and each separate background area is a one-piece group.**

Circle of Geese Variation Block

3

Drawing a Star Block with Odd Angles

Color blocks on page 123

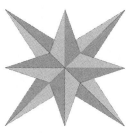

Star Block

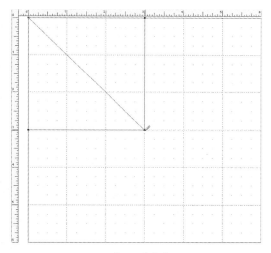

Steps 4 & 5

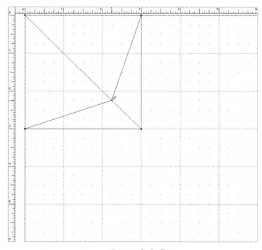

Steps 6 & 7

Here is a fun way to learn to draw with odd angles in EasyDraw™. First, we'll draw one-fourth of the block. Then, we'll clone and rotate to see a star magically appear. For all you paper piecing enthusiasts, this odd angle technique is a stepping stone to designing more complex paper piecing blocks.

1 On the BLOCK menu, point to New Block, click EasyDraw™. Turn Snap to Grid OFF, Snap to Node ON, Snap to Drawing OFF.

2 Also on the BLOCK menu, click Drawing Board Setup and enter these values:

General Tab
Snap to Grid Points
    Horizontal = 24   Vertical = 24
Block Size
    Horizontal = 6   Vertical = 6
Graph Paper Tab
Number of Divisions
    Horizontal = 6   Vertical = 6
Options
    Style = Graph paper lines

3 Click on the Line tool.

4 Draw a horizontal line starting at 3.00" from the top to the center of the block. Draw a vertical line starting at 3.00" from the left to the center of the block, creating a square in the upper-left quadrant.

5 Draw a diagonal line from the upper-left corner of the block to the center of the block.

6 Draw a line beginning at the top center and ending it on the diagonal line at 2 1/4".

7 Draw a line beginning at the left center and ending it on the diagonal line at 2 1/4".

3

8 Starting at the top-left corner, draw a line above the diagonal, extending it beyond the existing line and ending it on the grid point at 1 3/4" from the top and 2 3/4" from the left.

9 Draw a line below the diagonal from the top-left corner, mirroring the first, and ending it on the grid point at 2 3/4" from the top and 1 3/4" from the left.

It looks strange at this stage, but keep going. Many times when you are drawing a paper pieced block in EasyDraw™, this is the only way to accomplish the odd angles. We have to draw lines that extend beyond existing ones.

10 Save the block in the Sketchbook, then click on the Refresh button.

Notice how EQ5 neatly cropped off the excess part of the lines and added a node where the lines intersect. Without using any of the advanced drawing features, we are able to draw a block with odd angles. EQ5 will magically clean up the excess lines for you – including any duplicate lines that are on top of each other when you clone and rotate.

3

\ **Tip** ————————————————
- **The real advantage of drawing odd angled lines this way is that they are adjustable. You can use the Edit tool, select the line you want to adjust, and then grab the end node and move it to a new grid point.**

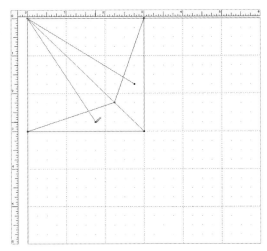
Steps 8 & 9

Step 10
Refresh Button

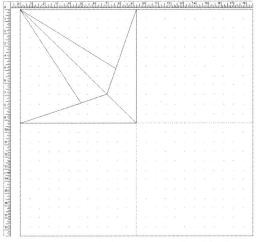
Lines cropped after saving in Sketchbook.

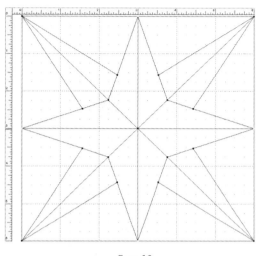

Step 13

Completed Star Block

Using the basics you just learned, create your own "mystery" star block. Try different angles or try something different with the central design. You could also design the quarter block as the entire block and then play with rotations on the quilt itself.

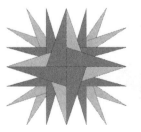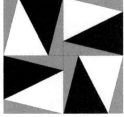

11 Click on the small black square in the corner of the Select tool to open the Symmetry box.

12 On the EDIT menu, click on Select All (or CTRL+A).

13 On the Symmetry box, click Clone, then click Rot 90. Move the cloned section to the upper-right quadrant, aligning the nodes carefully and making sure it snaps into place when you release the mouse. *Keep the newest section selected,* then repeat Clone and Rot 90 two more times, moving each new section to its respective quadrant to complete the block.

14 Click on the Save in Sketchbook button to save your block.

3

Drawing a Complex Paper Pieced Pattern

*Color block
on page 124*

Practice your drawing skills on this toy tractor block to learn how to develop a complex foundation pattern for paper piecing. We'll also be using EQ5's tracing feature which will make our task much easier!

To prepare yourself for drawing this block, I recommend you work through two previous exercises in this book: *Drawing a Simple Paper Piecing Block* on page 24 and *Drawing a Star Block with Odd Angles* on page 159.

Paper Pieced Tractor

Getting the Picture

First, we need a picture to trace. In this exercise we're going to use an appliqué block already in the EQ Block Library. We'll use the Snapshot feature in EQ5 to quickly convert the block into a Windows bitmap and then we'll bring it back into EQ5 for tracing.

Using an appliqué block from EQ5 is just one way to get a picture for tracing, and of course, I knew that everyone would already have it! You can also *scan* your own copyright-free photographs, line drawings, or sketches for tracing in EQ5. Another way to get pictures is to use a *digital camera*. A digital camera will save you several steps as opposed to scanning, since the images can be loaded directly into your computer. Use Windows Paint™ or any other image editing software to convert your images to a Windows bitmap to import for tracing.

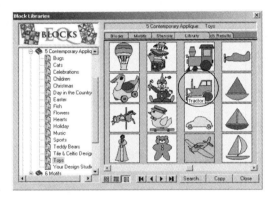

*Step 1
Retrieve the Tractor Block*

1   Retrieve the block named Tractor from the EQ5 Block Library, under Contemporary Appliqué / Toys.

2   Click on the View Sketchbook button, and on the Blocks tab. Select the Tractor block, then click the Edit button to place the block on the worktable.

Step 3

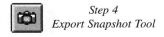

Step 4
Export Snapshot Tool

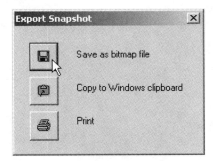

Step 6

Step 3

3 Click on the Color tab so you can export this block in color for easier tracing. You can use the default coloring or recolor it. Pale solids work best for visibility.

4 Click on the Export Snapshot tool.

5 Point the cursor just above the upper-left corner of the block, and draw a selection box around the entire block, then release the mouse.

6 After you release the mouse, the Export Snapshot box will appear. Click Save as bitmap file.

7 Navigate to the folder where you want to save the file by clicking on the down arrow beside Save in. Type a name in the box beside File name and then click on Save.

Building the Foundation

1 On the BLOCK menu, point to New Block, click EasyDraw™. Turn Snap to Grid ON, Snap to Node ON, Snap to Drawing OFF.

2 Also on the BLOCK menu, click Drawing Board Setup and enter these values:

General Tab
Snap to Grid Points
    Horizontal = 96   Vertical = 96
Block Size
    Horizontal = 6   Vertical = 6
Graph Paper Tab
Number of Divisions
    Horizontal = 6   Vertical = 6
Options
    Style = Graph paper lines

3 On the BLOCK menu, click Import for Tracing.

3

4 In the Import for Tracing box, navigate to where you saved the tractor bitmap, click the file to select it, then click Open. This adds the tractor image to the drawing board for you to trace. It should be a perfect fit since we exported it from there to begin with!

⟋ **Tip** ────────────────

• **If the imported bitmap does not fit within the drawing board exactly, you can adjust its placement by clicking on the crosshairs in the center and dragging it to fit.**

5 Click on the EasyDraw™ tab.

6 Click on the Line tool.

Remember when creating a paper piecing pattern, you need to work from the larger to the smaller. Study the tractor picture for a moment and visually divide the block into sections. I'll show you how I decided to divide up the block, but you just have to make your best guess and then go with it!

7 Start by drawing a diagonal dividing line from the top of the block to the bottom, following the angle of the windshield of the tractor. If you don't get the angle right on the first try, don't undo it, just re-adjust it. Use the Edit tool, select the line and grab the end nodes to readjust, making sure the end nodes still fall on the block outline.

⟋ **Tip** ────────────────

• **You can easily toggle between the Edit tool and the Line tool by pressing the Spacebar on your keyboard.**

8 Draw lines to further subdivide these first two sections, making sure that your lines intersect with existing lines *or* are connected to the block outline. Click on the Hide/Show bitmap button to see what your drawing looks like so far.

Step 7

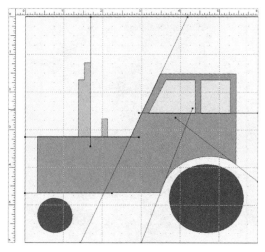

Step 8

 Hide/Show Bitmap button

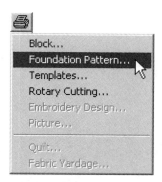

Check your Piece-ability under Foundation Pattern

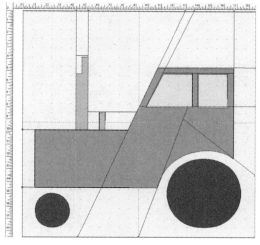

Step 10

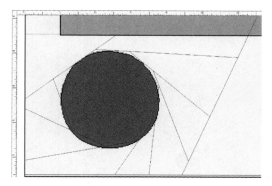

Step 11

9 Once you are satisfied, save the block in the Sketchbook.

Check your Piece-ability!

Click on the Print button and select Foundation Pattern. Click on the Sections tab to see if EQ5 has been able to compute your piecing sections. If it has, it will be indicated by the blue dotted lines. If you do not see these blue lines, that means EQ cannot compute a piecing order for your drawing and you will need to redraw the sections.

If EQ5 cannot compute a piecing order from your drawing, it will actually tell you so. If your block is ok, the Section tab will come up first when you go to Print Foundation Pattern. If there is a problem, the Numbering tab comes up first and you'll get a message like, "This block has a curve..." or "This block has an inside corner..."

I highly recommend that you *save your block in the Sketchbook and check your "piece-ability" after you complete **each** section.* If you encounter a problem along the way with piecing, you will have a general idea where to look for the problem and you can easily go back a step to redraw.

10 Working in each of the new sections separately, further subdivide the block to define the tractor's shape. Leave the sections with the tires until last. I generally start where I see the obvious lines and work my way to the more difficult.

11 Now let's do the tires. First, turn off Snap to Grid. It's much easier to draw around a circular shape if you turn off the Snap to Grid.

⬐ Tip

• **Try turning on the Snap to Drawing feature temporarily to get the line where you need it.**

165

12 To draw the circular shapes, we still use straight lines. In the section with the tire, draw a line that connects two adjacent sides of the section and that just barely touches part of the circle. Then working in a clockwise (or counterclockwise) direction, draw lines around the circle in sort of a loose spiral manner as illustrated.

Start each new line beyond the previous one. End it beyond the side of the section you are drawing towards. Work your way around the circle until you get back near where you began, and then draw the last lines intersecting them with your initial line if necessary.

Drawing around circles will get easier with practice. Don't worry if your circle only has a few points, this is the nature of paper piecing. Remember that you are going to be sewing this block, so don't get too particular – the more lines you add to make a near perfect circle, the tinier the pieces get!

13 Save your block in the Sketchbook. Check your piece-ability one last time to make sure everything is in good sewing order!

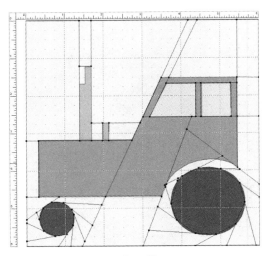

Step 12

Tip

- **Turn OFF Snap to Grid to accomplish difficult odd angles.**

- **If you encounter a tight spot, try turning ON Snap to Drawing temporarily to get the line where you need it. I do *not* recommend drawing the entire block with this feature on.**

- **Occasionally, click on the Hide/Show Bitmap button to see your block without the bitmap.**

- **EQ5 is pretty good at defining the sections and piecing order, but remember you can always regroup the sections if you like.**

How far can you take EQ5 in designing complex paper piecing designs? If you are very careful about saving in steps and checking the "piece-ability", there is no end to the paper piecing pattern potential!

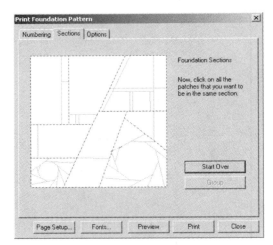

Make sure your Foundation Sections suit your needs.

Completed Paper Pieced Tractor

3

Drawing a Rolling Stone Block

Color blocks on page 124

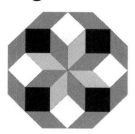

Rolling Stone Block

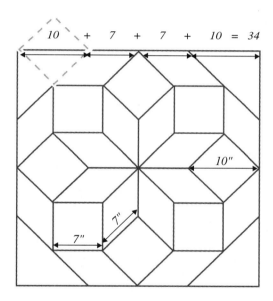

10 + 7 + 7 + 10 = 34

10"

7"

7"

The Rolling Stone block is popular not only as a block by itself, but also as a layout for whole quilts. Let's walk through how to determine the Snap to Grid points. If you have not read the *Secret Patch Code of the LeMoyne Star* on page 32, do so now or this may not make sense!

Finding the Grid

The first thing we need to do is total the parts that fall along the edge of the block. This total will be the number of Snap to Grid points we need to type in the Drawing Board Setup.

In the Rolling Stone block, you can see the diamonds that make up the eight-point star in the center. It's just like the LeMoyne Star with squares on-point between the diamonds at the top, bottom, and sides. To calculate the total on one side of the block, use these variables:

- All sides of diamonds = 7 grid points
- All sides of Squares = 7 grid points
- Diagonals of all squares = 10 grid points

The illustration shows how I added the total along the top of the block. Now let's draw the block and learn more tricks to make it easier.

Drawing the Block

1   On the BLOCK menu, point to New Block, click EasyDraw™. Turn Snap to Grid ON, Snap to Node ON, Snap to Drawing OFF.

2   Also on the BLOCK menu, click Drawing Board Setup and enter these values:

General Tab
Snap to Grid Points
    Horizontal = 34   Vertical = 34
Block Size
    Horizontal = 34   Vertical = 34
Graph Paper Tab
Number of Divisions
    Horizontal = 17   Vertical = 17
Options
    Style = Graph paper lines

3

For the graph paper divisions, we could also enter 34 x 34, but having that many lines on the Drawing Board is hard on the eyes. Just remember with the divisions set at 17, every graph paper square is equal to 2.00".

3   Click on the Line tool.

The first step is to create a few guidelines on the block. Guidelines take the guesswork out of drawing a block with an unusual grid. With the guidelines in place, you will be able to see exactly where to start and end a line.

4   Draw three horizontal lines across the block at these ruler markings: 5.00", 10.00" and 12.00" from the top. Next draw one vertical line at 17.00" (top center) to the center point of the block.

5   Click on the small black square in the corner of the Select tool to open the Symmetry box.

6   On the EDIT menu, click on Select All (or CTRL+A).

7   On the Symmetry box, click Clone and then click Rot 90. Move the cloned lines to the right side of the block, making sure that they snap into place correctly.

8   *While the new section is still selected*, repeat the Clone and Rot 90 two more times, moving each clone into its respective part of the block. It should look like the illustration for this step.

9   Click on the Save in Sketchbook button to save your guideline block. Take a moment to add information on the Notecard, so that you will remember what it's for.

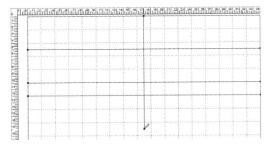

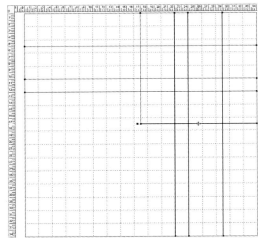

Step 4

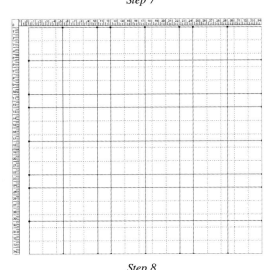

Step 7

Step 8

3

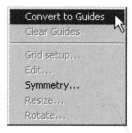

Step 10

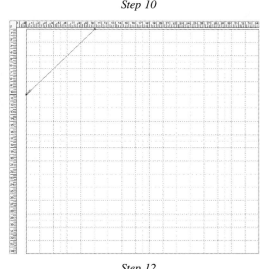

Step 12

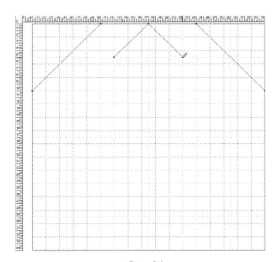

Step 14

10 Once the block is saved, right-click on the drawing board and click on Convert to Guides.

11 Click on the Line tool

Sometimes it may seem difficult to know where to begin drawing the block. I usually begin in the upper-left corner or choose a part of the block that I know is easy to place. Since this block fits together like a puzzle, once you establish one of the pieces, the rest will fall into place. You will be amazed at how the guidelines will help!

We will make our work even easier by *drawing only the top half of the block* and then we can clone and flip it to complete the block.

12 Let's begin by drawing the diagonal lines that form the triangles in the upper-left and upper-right corners. Draw a diagonal line from right to left beginning at the top of the block, 10.00" from the left, and ending it 10.00" from the top on the left side of the block.

13 Draw a mirror image diagonal line in the upper-right corner. Beginning at the top of the block at 24.00" from the left and ending it at 10.00" from the top on the right side of the block.

Remember to use the guidelines when you draw and you will not have to worry about numbers on the ruler. The ruler positions are included here in part just for the ease of writing the directions.

14 Draw two diagonal lines in opposite directions beginning at the top center and ending 5.00" from the top of the block. The left line ends on the grid point at 12.00" from the left and the right line ends at 22.00". These lines form the opposite sides of the diamonds along the top of the block.

3

15 Next, draw the lines that will complete the squares between the diamond patches, using the guidelines and the illustration at the right to help you. You only need to draw half of the on-point squares that fall on the center line of the block, as shown.

16 Now finish the top half of the block by drawing the remaining lines that form the diamonds in the center of the block as shown. Hint: All lines begin on a corner node of the squares and end in the center of the block. The top half of our block is now complete.

17 Click on the small black square in the corner of the Select tool to open the Symmetry box.

18 On the EDIT menu click on Select All (or CTRL+A).

19 On the Symmetry box, click on Clone and then click on Flip V.

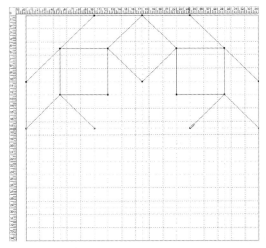

Step 15

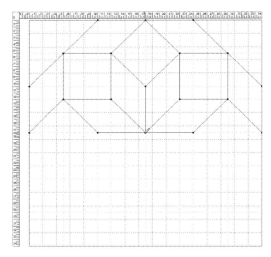

Step 16

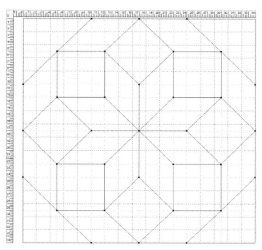

Step 20

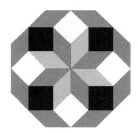

Completed Rolling Stone Block

Variation 1

Variation 2

20 *While the cloned half is still selected,* move it to the bottom half of the block, lining up the nodes and making sure it snaps into place.

21 Click in the Save to Sketchbook button to save your block.

Tip

• **Did you find the guidelines helpful? We drew them at significant points based on the 7 – 10 – 7 Secret Patch Code. We also used another number to draw the guidelines – the number 5. It's not an addition to the formula; it's just equal to half of the diagonal of the square. It comes in handy when we are drawing the on-point squares.**

Now that you have this great block in your Sketchbook, why not take it further and create your own unique variations?

The first variation was made by partitioning the diamonds. This is actually a traditional block pattern called, Ring around the Star. If you need more information on partitioning diamonds, see the *Drawing a Lone Star Block* exercise on page 86.

Think beyond the block and look at the Rolling Stone as an overall quilt layout. The second variation made use of partitioning too, but with added arcs to make little sun blocks between the diamonds. I'm sure you are already thinking of more variations, so have fun with it!

3

Chapter 4 Color Illustrations

Radiant Star
Page 180

Radiant Star Variation
Page 180

Radiant Star Variation
Page 180

Giant Dahlia
Page 190

4

Curved Geese
Page 194

Node Select All Variation
Page 199

Perspective Window Frame Variation
Page 202

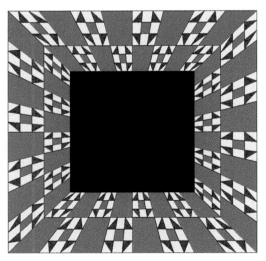

Perspective Window Frame Variation
Page 202

Perspective Window Frame Variation
Page 202

Perspective Window Frame Variation
Page 202

Hexagonal Star
Page 212

Hexagonal Star Variation
Page 212

4

Hexagonal Star Variation
Page 212

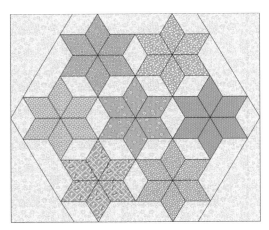

Seven Sisters
Page 216

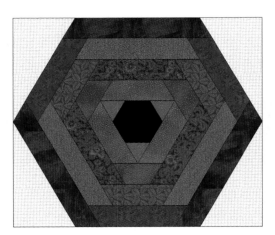

Log Cabin Hexagon
Page 218

Pineapple Geese
Page 218

4

Very Advanced Drawing

Chapter 4

Chapter 4 Overview

If the exercises in this book were based on real physical exercises, this last chapter would be considered the Olympic trials. Many of the blocks I chose for this chapter are a result of inquiries in my on-line classes and through the Info-EQ mailing list. Users want to know if they can draw these complex blocks in EQ5 – yes, you can! Don't shy away from the longer lessons – they contain all the details you need to accomplish these blocks. The reward may be several really spectacular quilts!

4

Drawing a Radiant Star Block

Color blocks on page 173

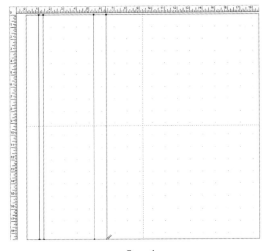

Radiant Star Block

Almost every national quilt show awards a prize to a Feathered Star quilt – that's how popular this pattern is! Besides that, it's also one of my favorites!

The block in this exercise is drawn in the standard 18 1/2" size with the feathers finishing at 1". It takes precise drawing, but once you have it drawn you will use it over and over again. In fact, after the block is completed, I will show you how to create variations in the center of the block. Let's get started!

1 On the BLOCK menu, point to New Block, click EasyDraw™. Turn Snap to Grid ON, Snap to Node ON, Snap to Drawing OFF.

2 Also on the BLOCK menu, click Drawing Board Setup and enter these values:

General Tab
Snap to Grid Points
    Horizontal = 148 Vertical = 148
Block Size
    Horizontal = 18.5 Vertical = 18.5
Graph Paper Tab
Number of Divisions
    Horizontal = 2   Vertical = 2
Options
    Style = Graph paper lines

First, we need to create some guidelines that will make this block much easier to draw.

3 Click on the Line tool.

4 Draw four vertical lines at these markings on the ruler:

1", 1 3/8", 5 3/8" and 6 3/8"

Zoom in to see the ruler markings better.

Step 4

5 Click on the small black square in the corner of the Select tool to open the Symmetry box.

6 Select all four lines by using CTRL+A.

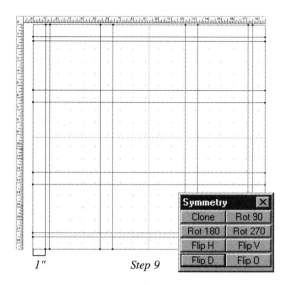

Step 9

1"

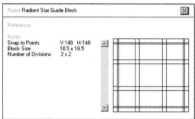

Record block specifics in notecard

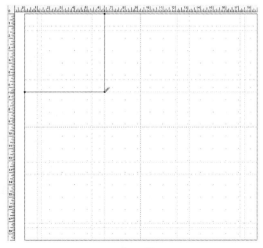

Step 13

7 On the Symmetry box, click on Clone. Then, while the cloned lines are still selected, click on Rot 90. Drag these lines to the top of the block *parking them carefully* so that the top line is 1" from the top of the block and a 1" square is formed in the upper-left corner.

8 Again, use CTRL+A to select all the lines.

9 On the Symmetry box, click on Clone, then click on Rot 180. Drag the cloned lines to the bottom-right corner of the block, *parking them carefully* and making sure they snap into place. Your finished guideline block should look like the illustration to the left. The four squares in the corners should measure 1".

10 Click on Save in Sketchbook to save your guideline block.

Tip ─────────────────────

- **Take time to add information on the Notecard! Name the block, "Radiant Star Guide Block," and then under Notes, add the snap points, block size, and any other information you want.**

- **Why 148 snap points? This is a case where I knew the size of the patches and the finished size of the standard block. In order to draw this block, I needed to be able to go down to an eighth of an inch (18.50" x 8 = 148 grid points).**

11 With the guideline block still on the drawing board, right-click and choose Convert to Guides on the context menu.

12 Click on the Line tool.

13 Following the guidelines, draw two lines to form a 6 3/8" square in the upper-left corner of the block.

Tip ─────────────────────

- **Use the Zoom tool if you have trouble zeroing in on the right spot.**

4

14 Draw two lines to form a 5 3/8" square inside the first one, ending them on the lines of the 6 3/8" square so they intersect each other. This creates a 1" square where the lines intersect.

15 Click on the small black square in the corner of the Select tool to open the Symmetry box.

16 Use CTRL+A to select all the lines.

17 On the Symmetry box, click on Clone. Then click on Rot 90. Drag the cloned lines to the upper-right corner, making sure they snap into place.

18 Repeat Clone and Rot 90 two more times, parking each clone carefully into its respective corner.

19 Click Save in Sketchbook.

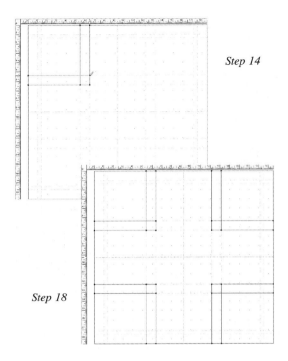

Step 14

Step 18

Now we have the four corners of the block established, but we need to create this same configuration on the diagonal between the star points. This is where we will use the EasyDraw™ arcs as our compass!

20 Click on the Arc tool.

21 Working counterclockwise from the top-left corner, draw an arc from the lower-right node of the 5 3/8" square to the corresponding node in the lower-left corner. Draw three more arcs in the same manner to complete the circle.

22 Draw four more arcs going from node to node in the block center as illustrated.

DO NOT SAVE IN SKETCHBOOK YET!
We only need the arcs temporarily to establish a center point for our diagonal lines and we do not want to create nodes where we don't need them. If you forget and save it, go back to the block we saved in Step 19 and redraw the arcs.

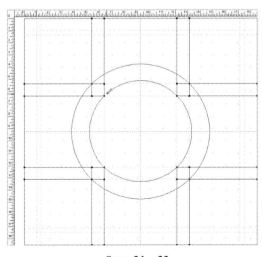

Steps 21 – 22

4

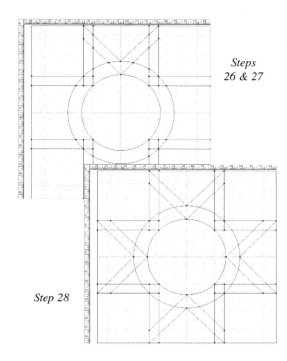

*Steps
26 & 27*

Step 28

23 Click on the small black square in the corner of the Edit tool to open the Edit Arc box.

24 To place a node at the center of each arc, click on each arc separately, then click on Half on the Edit Arc box.

25 Click on the Line tool.

The next two steps are more difficult to describe than they are to draw. Please look at the illustrations for help. When these diagonal lines are drawn, they will create the 45 degree diamonds at the tip of the star points.

26 Draw two diagonal lines forming a V-shape from the 5 3/8" corner square to the center node of the outer arcs. See illustration.

27 Draw two diagonal lines to form a second V-shape beneath the first from the center node of the inner arc to the guideline that is 1 3/8" from the block outline. You must be very precise; making sure the end of your diagonal line is parked exactly where the guideline intersects the solid line. Zooming in on the section will help.

28 Repeat step 27 three more times to draw each of the three other V-shapes.

29 Click Save in Sketchbook to create nodes.

30 Click on the Select tool. Select and delete all of the arcs.

31 Select and delete the short lines that extend from the diamonds to the block outline so that you have a nice quarter-square triangle between the star points.

32 Click on the Line tool again.

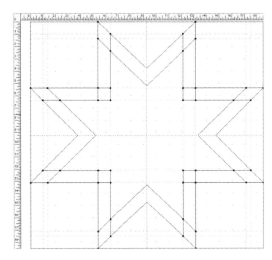

*Steps 30 & 31
Delete all of the arcs. Delete all of the short
lines between diamond and block outline.*

4

33 Notice that there are eight nodes on the points around the inside of the block. Skipping every other node, draw four lines to make a square by connecting the nodes. Then, draw a second square on point, connecting the remaining nodes in the center. This creates the octagon in the center and forms the kite-shaped star points.

34 Save your block in the Sketchbook. The hard part is done!

35 You can also remove the guidelines at this time. Right-click on the drawing board and choose Clear Guides.

36 Press the Refresh button to see your block correctly.

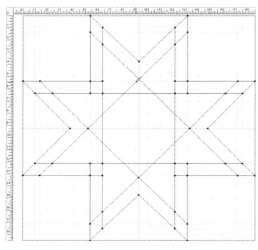

Step 33

Now it's time for the "feathers" in this "Feathered Star". These are actually the little half-square triangles. There are 48 of them. But don't worry, they *are* small and you'll be done with your masterpiece before you know it!

37 Click on the small black square in the corner of the Edit tool to open the Edit Line box.

38 On the Edit Line box, change the number beside Partition to 4.

39 Select each of the diagonal lines (the V-shapes) between the star points *separately,* then on the Edit Line box, click on Partition. Sorry, but you cannot multiple-select lines to partition.

40 Select each of the inside lines of the four corner squares, click on Partition again, partitioning them into four segments also.

41 For the remaining lines along the star points, select each and click on Thirds on the Edit Line box.

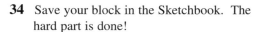

Partition = 4   Thirds

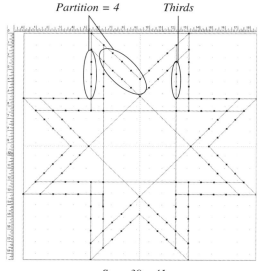

Steps 39 – 41

4

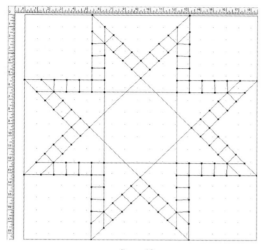

Step 43

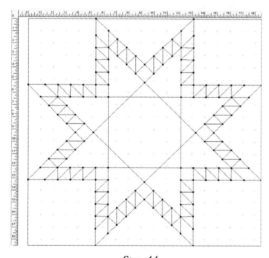

Step 44

Completed Radiant Star Block

42 Click on the Line tool, then *turn OFF Snap to Grid.*

43 Draw lines to connect the nodes between the newly segmented lines, creating squares along the kite-shaped star points.

44 Now go back and draw the remaining lines to divide each of the little squares into half-square triangles. The top of the feathers face away from the center towards the diamond points.

45 Click Save in Sketchbook.

Congratulations, your Radiant Star is finished! Pat yourself on the back, take a coffee break, and have a cookie. When you're refreshed, come back to the computer, I've got more to show you!

Tip

- Be sure to save your new Radiant Star in the User Libraries! (Pages 14 – 17 in Chapter 2)

- With your Radiant Star on the worktable, click on the Print button, then select Foundation Pattern. Look on the Sections tab and behold...your Radiant Star has paper piece-ability! On the Options tab, type in a size, click on Preview and take a look at how EQ has performed its magic. You could actually make a mini Radiant Star, if you like a challenge!

- If you do *not* see the blue lines showing the sections, then you will need to go back and check your drawing. Check the foundation pattern at the different stages of the block that were saved and try to pinpoint where you need to redraw.

4

Center Variations for the Radiant Star

These are just a few of the possible variations for the Radiant Star block. Use these for inspiration and create even more of your own. Perhaps you will create a prize-winning quilt!

To work on these variations, I recommend you begin a new project file. If you did not save your Radiant Star in the User Library, do so now so that you can use it in other projects.

As we work through these steps, zoom in on the center of the Radiant Star. Think of the center of the block as a very unique drawing board. We'll draw the centers using the nodes only, so *turn OFF Snap to Grid*.

Variation 1 – Peaceful Hours

This one is easy because we can use a connect-the-dot method to draw the star in the center. Draw lines to connect the nodes in the order illustrated. Save in Sketchbook.

Variation 2 – LeMoyne/Rolling Star

Place the block created in Variation 1 on the drawing board. Delete all the intersecting lines in the center of the star. Draw lines across the center of the star to form the eight diamond shapes for the LeMoyne Star. Save in Sketchbook. To make the center look like the Rolling Star block, delete the lines between the star points. Save in Sketchbook.

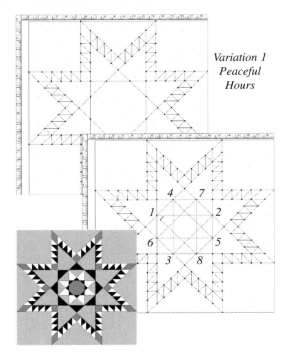

*Variation 1
Peaceful
Hours*

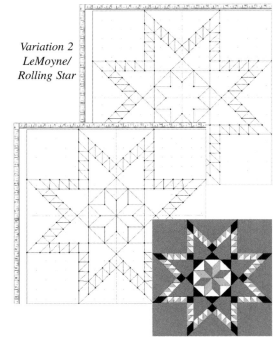

*Variation 2
LeMoyne/
Rolling Star*

4

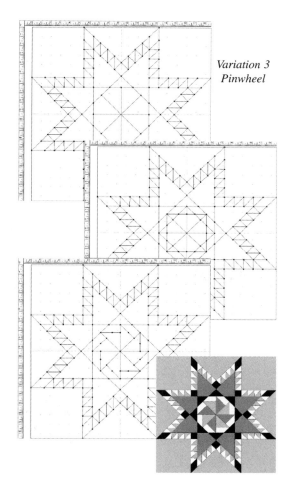

Variation 3
Pinwheel

Variation 3 – Pinwheel

To create a pinwheel block in the center, use the Edit Line box and partition each side of the center octagon in half. Connect these new nodes with lines dividing the octagon into eight equal slices.

Again, using these same nodes, draw a square and an on-point square. Save in Sketchbook to establish nodes. Decide which direction you want your pinwheel to face, then delete lines so the pinwheel's triangles all go in one direction.

4

Variation 4 – Pinwheel in a Star

Start with the block created in Variation 2.
Draw the square and on-point square as for the
Pinwheel. Save in Sketchbook, then delete
lines within the star to create the pinwheel.

Variation 5 – Kaleidoscope

Delete the eight lines that form the octagon in
the center. Draw lines across the center to
create eight equal blades. Draw straight lines
across the kite-shaped star points between each
blade.

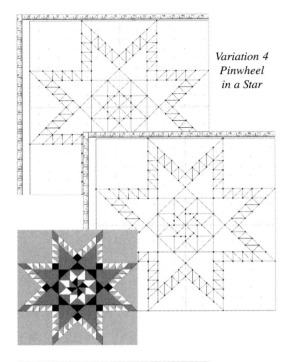

*Variation 4
Pinwheel
in a Star*

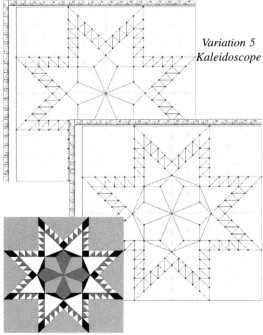

*Variation 5
Kaleidoscope*

4

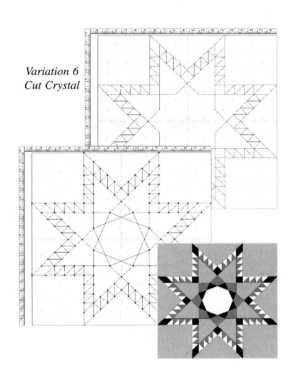

Variation 6
Cut Crystal

Variation 6 – Cut Crystal

Delete the lines of the center octagon. Draw two tilted squares using the nodes on the kites. Save in Sketchbook.

Variations 7 & 8 – Your turn!

Now here's a little test for you. Draw these last two variations using the Cut Crystal center, practicing what you have learned.

Variation 7

Variation 8

4

Drawing a Giant Dahlia Block

Color block on page 173

The Giant Dahlia block is actually meant to be made as a whole quilt. Drawing it in EQ5 will give you precision templates for making it. Even if you never *sew* one of these beauties, the skills you learn as you draw it will be very helpful for other challenging blocks.

Giant Dahlia Block

1   On the BLOCK menu, point to New Block, click EasyDraw™. Turn Snap to Grid ON, Snap to Node ON, Snap to Drawing OFF.

2   Also on the BLOCK menu, click Drawing Board Setup and enter these values:

   General Tab
   Snap to Grid Points
        Horizontal = 48   Vertical = 48
   Block Size
        Horizontal = 12   Vertical = 12
   Graph Paper Tab
   Number of Divisions
        Horizontal = 12   Vertical = 12
   Options
        Style = Graph paper lines

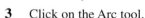**Tip** ─────────────────────────

• **We'll be drawing the Giant Dahlia as a 12" block, but remember, you can print it any size you need for templates.**

3   Click on the Arc tool.

4   Measuring in from the block outline, draw three circles (four arcs each) at 1/2", 4 1/2" and 4 3/4". Once you have the circles drawn, you can turn off the graph paper lines.

5   Click on the small black square on the Edit tool to open the Edit Arc box.

6   On the Edit Arc box, change the numbers beside Partition and Stagger to 4.

7   Select each arc of the outermost and the second largest circle separately, then on the Edit Arc box click on Partition.

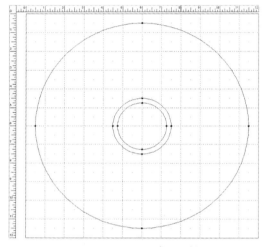

Step 4

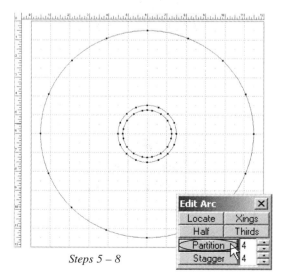

Steps 5 – 8

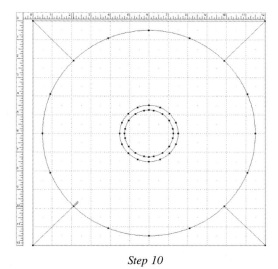

Step 10

8 Select each of the arcs of the innermost circle, then click on Stagger.

9 Click on the Line tool.

10 Draw diagonal lines from each corner of the block to the corresponding node at 45 degrees on the outer circle.

11 Click on the Save in Sketchbook button.

⟍Tip ─────────────────────────

• **Whenever you have a circle that is floating inside the block, you need to add at least two anchor lines to attach it to the block outline. These can be drawn on the diagonal like this block, or at the center top, bottom or on the sides. EQ5 needs these anchor lines to define the background patches correctly.**

12 Turn OFF Snap to Grid.

Notice that the Giant Dahlia's center is a small Dresden Plate. We'll draw that first. Zoom in on the center to make it easier to see.

13 Draw sixteen lines from the nodes on the innermost circle to the center of the block, ignoring the nodes where the arcs connect.

14 Draw the triangle points on top of each blade going in a zigzag manner between the nodes of two of the circles.

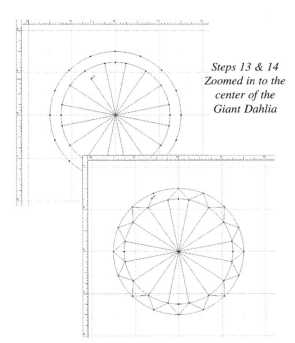

Steps 13 & 14 Zoomed in to the center of the Giant Dahlia

4

15 Click on the Select tool. Select and delete all of the arcs of the innermost circle only. Leave the remaining arcs around the Dresden Plate center until we create the petals of our dahlia. Removing them too soon makes the block unstable. Zoom out to see the entire block.

16 Click on the Save in Sketchbook button.

The spiral design of the Giant Dahlia is created by drawing overlapping petal shapes. It's not difficult, but it can be confusing to the eyes! Work in a clockwise manner to keep from getting confused.

17 Click on the Arc tool.

18 Beginning at point 1 (see illustration) on the Dresden Plate center, draw an arc to node 2 at 12 o'clock on the outer circle. (Press your keyboard spacebar if the arc is flipped the wrong direction.) Draw a second arc from point 2 to point 3 on the center circle. Note that the arcs begin and end *every sixth node* on the Dresden Plate center.

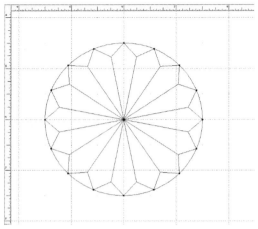

Step 15
Zoomed in to center of Giant Dahlia

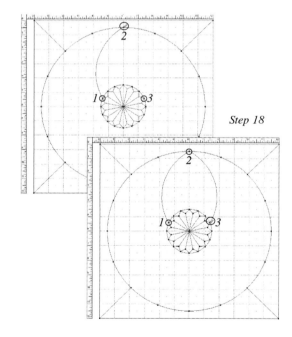

Step 18

4

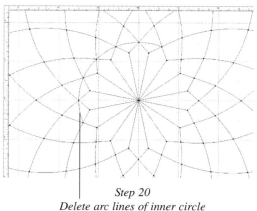

Step 19

Step 20
Delete arc lines of inner circle

19 Draw a second petal, beginning at the next clockwise point of the center and ending six points away. Continue drawing this way, clockwise, until you have drawn all 16 petals.

You will begin to see a spiral pattern once you get around to about 9 o'clock. Look back at your drawing after every few petals, and if the spiral seems askew, you may need to delete and redraw some of the petals.

20 When you have finished drawing all sixteen petals, zoom in and delete the arcs between the Dresden points.

21 Save your finished Giant Dahlia in the Sketchbook.

Variations and Ideas...

One of the things I like best about this block is how fun it is to color. Try using a shaded palette of solid colors. Or, create your own shaded palette of batiks and marbled fabrics from the EQ5 Fabric Library.

Why not add one more round of petals? On the outer circle, partition each arc segment between the petals in half. Draw arcs for the *new* petals beginning at the nodes created, to the outermost intersection of the existing petals. Save to Sketchbook, and then go back and delete the arc segments that are not needed.

Try a different center, or leave just a plain circle in the middle. Try fewer or more petals. In other words...have fun with it!

Completed
Giant Dahlia

Giant Dahlia
Variation

4

Drawing Curved Geese

*Color block
on page 174*

This exercise will show you how to make your geese fly in curves! The block has a nice smooth curve that will repeat if set in a border or if you want your geese to fly across the quilt.

1 On the BLOCK menu, point to New Block, click EasyDraw™. Turn Snap to Grid ON, Snap to Node ON, Snap to Drawing OFF.

2 Also on the BLOCK menu, click Drawing Board Setup and enter these values:

General Tab

Snap to Grid Points

    Horizontal = 24   Vertical = 48

Block Size

    Horizontal = 6   Vertical = 12

Graph Paper Tab

Number of Divisions

    Horizontal = 6   Vertical = 12

Options

    Style = Graph paper lines

3 Click on the Arc tool.

In the next three steps, press your keyboard spacebar before releasing the mouse to make the arc flip in the opposite direction as needed.

4 Draw a right-facing arc beginning at the top of the block 1" from the left to the graph paper intersection at 2" horizontal and 3" vertical.

5 Draw a second arc, this time left-facing, beginning at the end node of the first arc and ending at 2" horizontal and 9" vertical.

Curved Geese

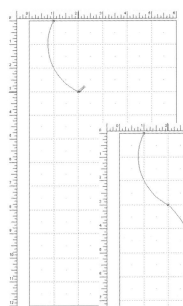

Steps 4 & 5

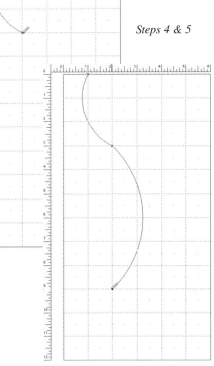

4

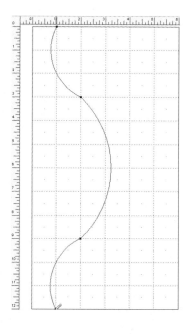

Step 6

Step 7
Edit Tool

Steps 8 & 9

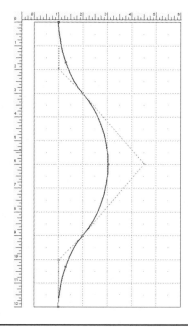

6 Draw a third arc, again right-facing, from the end node of the second arc to the bottom of the block, 1" from the left.

Notice that the central arc is *twice* as long as the top and bottom arcs. If you are trying to create a repeating curve, this is important to remember.

Although this initial curve is symmetrical, it's not smooth. If you set this block end to end, you would end up with a V-shape where the lines meet. To fix this, we need to smooth our curve so it is contained within a two-inch column. The graph paper lines make this easy.

7 Click on the Edit tool.

8 Hold down the keyboard SHIFT key and select the top and bottom arc so that you can see the handle tent on both at the same time. Click the top arc's handle and drag it to the right 1", so it is parallel to the top node. Repeat this with the bottom arc, making it a mirror image of the top arc.

9 Select the center arc. Drag the handle to the left so that the arc's center rests on the 3" line. Be sure it stays on the vertical center line (6" from the top).

Now we have a nice smooth symmetrical curve that will repeat well if we set the blocks in a border.

4

⎇ Tip

- **Although we can build smooth curves with arcs, remember that in EasyDraw™ they are *still* separate arcs. They can easily separate at the nodes, so you must be careful to keep them connected.**

- **Save this block at different stages as we go through the exercise so that you can play with variations later on.**

10 Click on the Select tool. Then use CTRL+A to select all arcs.

11 Click on Copy (CTRL+C). Then click on Paste (CTRL+V). Drag the new curve two inches to the right so the top and bottom nodes are at 3" from the left. Make sure it snaps into place on the grid.

12 Click the Save in Sketchbook button.

13 Click on the small black square in the corner of the Edit tool, to open the Edit Arc box.

14 Click on each of the two top arcs separately. Then click on Thirds on the Edit Arc box. Repeat with the bottom two arcs.

15 On the Edit Arc box, change the number beside Partition to 6.

16 Click on each of the center arcs separately. Then click on Partition.

17 Click on the Line tool. Draw horizontal lines from node to node between the two curves. At this stage, it looks like a curvy ladder.

4

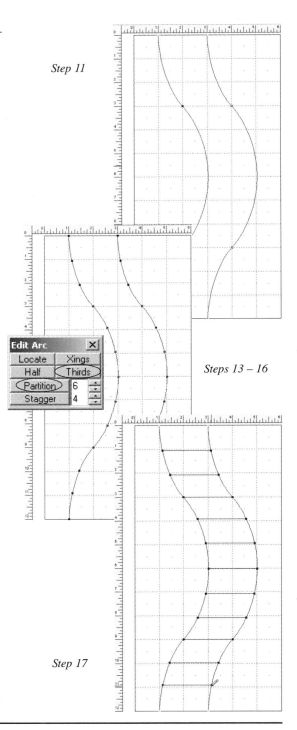

Step 11

Steps 13 – 16

Step 17

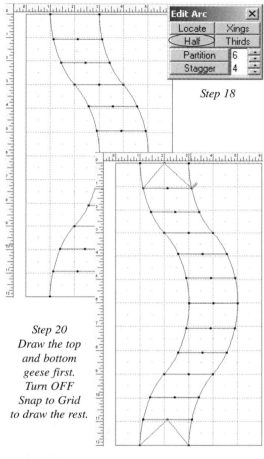

Step 18

Step 20
Draw the top
and bottom
geese first.
Turn OFF
Snap to Grid
to draw the rest.

18 Click on the Edit tool again, bringing up the Edit Arc box. Click on each horizontal line between the curves, and then on the Edit Arc box, click on Half.

19 Click on the Line tool.

20 Draw two diagonal lines to the center within each section of the ladder to create the triangular geese shape. All geese are flying to the North (points up).

✎ Tip ───────────────────────

• **Draw the diagonal lines for the top and bottom geese first. Then turn OFF Snap to Grid to do the rest. This will ensure that the ends snap to a grid point along the block outline.**

21 Once you have all the geese completed, Save in Sketchbook again.

This particular curved geese block works well for repeating border blocks, but you can use it in other ways too. Keep reading to learn how to make a matching corner block so your geese will fly in formation all around the quilt!

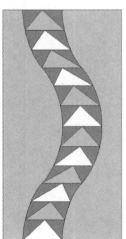

Completed Curved
Geese Block

4

To create a matching corner block, place a new EasyDraw™ block on the worktable. On the BLOCK menu, click Drawing Board Setup and enter these values:

General Tab

Snap to Grid Points

Horizontal = 24   Vertical = 24

Block Size

Horizontal = 6   Vertical = 6

Graph Paper Tab

Number of Divisions

Horizontal = 6   Vertical = 6

Options

Style = Graph paper lines

As illustrated, draw two arcs, partition each into 8 segments, then draw the geese triangles so they are flying to the East (points to the right).

Play around with building curves in EasyDraw™ and see what you come up with. Try varying the width at the top and bottom to get a three-dimensional effect. By the way…you can use this same idea to make a Curved Sawtooth block!

Tip

• **Make a foundation pattern! When you print it on the Sections tab, group all the pieces of the long geese curve together, then group each background patch separately. Renumbering the foundation is optional, since a long string of geese must always be paper pieced from the base to point anyway.**

Curved Geese Corner Block

Curved Geese 3D Variation

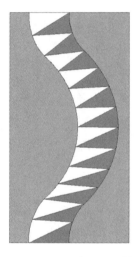

Curved Sawtooth Block Variation

Print a Foundation Pattern

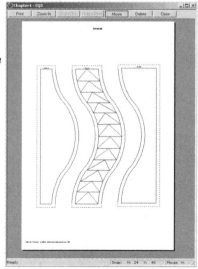

Exercising with Node Select All

Color block on page 174

Swirl Marble Block

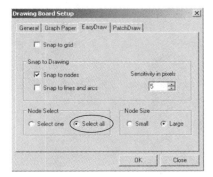

Step 2

Step 7
Arc Tool

A rarely used advanced drawing feature is the Node Select all. With this option selected, when you click on a node with the Edit tool, the node and all segments connected to it will be selected. This exercise is more for practice than for a particular block. Try the Swirl Marble block to learn how it works.

1 On the BLOCK menu, click on Drawing Board Setup.

2 Click on the EasyDraw™ tab. (You must have the Advanced drawing features enabled in the FILE menu Preferences to see this additional tab.)

3 Under Node Select, click the circle beside Select all.

4 Click OK.

⟍ Tip ⎯⎯⎯⎯⎯⎯⎯⎯⎯⎯⎯⎯⎯

• **On the EasyDraw™ tab of the Drawing Board Setup, you can leave both Select all and Large options on at all times. The larger nodes are easier to see. As for "Select all", you can click on individual segments, not the node, and move them independently.**

5 On the BLOCK menu, point to New Block, click EasyDraw™. Turn Snap to Grid ON, Snap to Node ON, Snap to Drawing OFF.

6 Also on the BLOCK menu, click Drawing Board Setup and enter these values:

General Tab
Snap to Grid Points
    Horizontal = 24   Vertical = 24
Block Size
    Horizontal = 6   Vertical = 6
Graph Paper Tab
Number of Divisions
    Horizontal = 6   Vertical = 6
Options
    Style = Graph paper lines

7 Click on the Arc tool.

4

8 Starting at the top center of the block, draw four arcs to make a circle that fills the block.

9 Click on the small black square in the corner of the Edit tool to open the Edit Arc box.

10 Click on each arc separately, and on the Edit Arc box, click on Thirds.

11 Click on the Arc tool. Draw twelve arcs from the nodes on the circle to the center of the block, having them all facing the same direction. Save in Sketchbook.

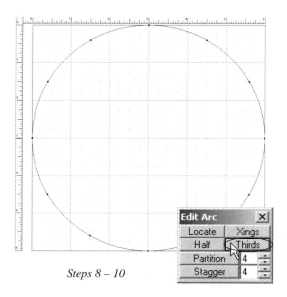

Steps 8 – 10

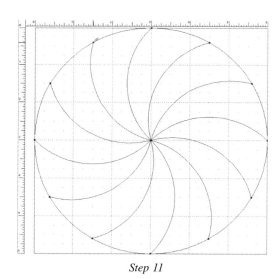

Step 11

4

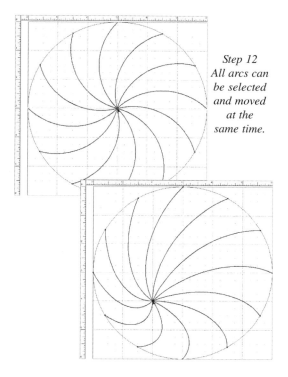

*Step 12
All arcs can
be selected
and moved
at the
same time.*

Now the fun begins!

12 Click on the Edit tool. Click on the node in the center. Notice that all of the arcs are selected too. Now drag the node to another grid point within the circle. All of the arcs will move with it.

Notice that the node you are moving around is still affected by Snap to Grid and Snap to Node. You can turn OFF Snap to Grid and make the center of your swirl anywhere you like, but don't get too carried away! Two rules:

1) All of the arcs should stay within the circle

2) Don't make the arcs bend so much that they cross back over each other.

Try other circle blocks with converging lines or arcs. Partition all the inner arcs and draw additional lines or make them into curved geese! Draw a smaller circle centered over the converging arcs, save it in the Sketchbook and then delete the segments within the circle for a button effect …or is that a hole?

Completed Block

*Variation 1
Curved Geese*

Variation 2

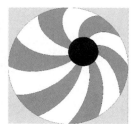

Variation 3

4

Drawing a Perspective Window Frame Block

Color blocks on page 174 – 175

Here's a really cool window-frame type block with lots of potential. The angles of the lines converge to a vanishing point, giving it the illusion of depth. It looks great around a landscape quilt, floral appliqué, or even a photo image. Instructions on how to use this in a quilt layout are at the end of the exercise.

If you do not have Node Select All turned on, please see the previous exercise, *Exercising with Node Select All* on page 199.

Perspective Window Frame Blocks

1 On the BLOCK menu, point to New Block, click EasyDraw™. Turn Snap to Grid ON, Snap to Node ON, Snap to Drawing OFF.

2 Also on the BLOCK menu, click Drawing Board Setup and enter these values:

> **General Tab**
> Snap to Grid Points
> > Horizontal = 24   Vertical = 24
>
> Block Size
> > Horizontal = 8   Vertical = 8
>
> **Graph Paper Tab**
> Number of Divisions
> > Horizontal = 8   Vertical = 8
>
> Options
> > Style = Graph paper lines

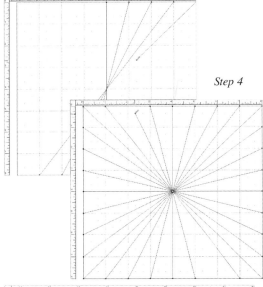

Step 4

3 Click on the Line tool.

4 Draw lines spaced 1" apart from the block outline to the center point of the block.

5 Save in Sketchbook. The center will look thick and dark even though there is only one node.

6 Now we're going to "cut" a window out of our block. Click on the Line tool.

7 Following the graph paper lines, draw a 4" square in the center of the block 2" in from the block outline (two graph paper squares).

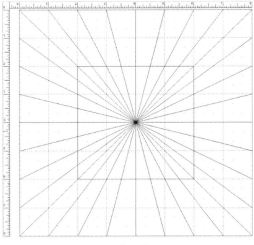

Step 7

4

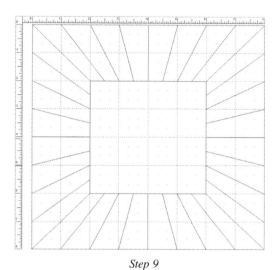

Step 9

Completed Frame Block

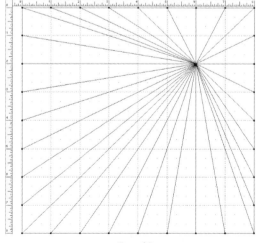

Step 13

8 Save in Sketchbook to establish nodes.

9 Click on the Select tool. Delete all the converging lines within the center square.

10 Save your new frame block in the Sketchbook.

Changing the Perspective

Now let's take the converging line block we saved in Step 5 and give our window a different point of view.

11 Retrieve the block saved in Step 5 and place it on the worktable.

12 Click on the Edit tool.

13 Click on the node in the center of the block and drag it up to the graph paper intersection at 6" horizontal and 2" vertical. Keep the lines stemming from the vanishing point straight if you want the block to have a window frame effect.

Voila! With the Node "Select all" feature turned on, we changed the horizon line and the vanishing point in one easy step!

4

14 Click on the Line tool. Draw a square around the vanishing point again. Look for where the lines that stem from the corners cross the graph paper intersections.

15 Save in Sketchbook to establish nodes and then delete all the lines within the square.

16 Save your finished block to the Sketchbook.

You can also draw rectangular windows, but you will need to experiment with block size and the divisions if you want to keep the frame effect (i.e. lines connecting the corners of the block and the window). You can also resize your square block into a rectangle in the quilt layout.

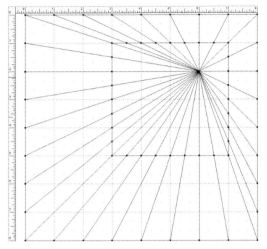

Step 14

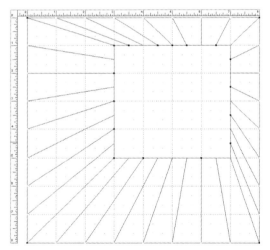

Step 15

Completed Frame Block

Variation 1
Using an oval window
and appliqué flowers

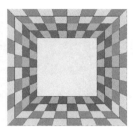

Variation 2
Lines create a
perspective grid

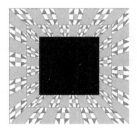

Variation 3
Perspective using blocks

Variation 4
Get creative using
blocks in a quilt layout

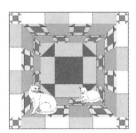

Variation 5
Customize your
perspective layout by
using appliqué motifs

Let's not forget circular and oval windows. They look great around appliqué flowers! You know how to create a circle with four arcs. To create an oval, draw four arcs as you would for a circle, but make two of the parallel sides closer together. When you first draw your oval, it will look something like a potato. To make a nice smooth oval, use the Edit tool, select the arcs and adjust the tent handle to make a right angle. (The illustration shows the oval without the converging lines so you can see what I did.)

You can divide the window frame further by drawing more lines to create a perspective grid. There are two examples of these in the EQ5 Block Library under Contemporary Pieced, Pinwheels & Potpourri. To do this, partition the corner lines only and then connect these with lines around the frame.

If you are really adventurous, you can further subdivide a perspective grid and make quilt blocks within the grid squares. Keep the blocks simple and you will be able to print a foundation pattern for your frame!

How to use the window block

Set the window frame block in a 1 x 1 Horizontal quilt layout on Layer 1 or use Custom Set. Custom Set will give you more flexibility because you can easily change the block proportions. Once you've set it in the quilt, switch to Layer 2 and place a block or imported picture over the window opening, adjusting the size to fit the window.

To increase the three-dimensionality, add a border with matching block divisions. On Layer 2, place blocks or pictures over the window opening. Add appliqué motifs in varying sizes to make it look like your quilt has depth. By the way…those cool cats are in the EQ5 Block Library under Contemporary Appliqué, Cats. The block I used is called Puss in the Corner.

4

Drawing a Base for Hexagonal Blocks

I saved hexagonal blocks for this last chapter because you have to think beyond the square drawing board, which goes against the normal way of drawing in EQ5. Hexagons are not hard to draw, they're just fussy about the way they fit together in a quilt! There are several ways to draw 60° blocks in EQ5. The method you use depends on what you want to do with the block. In this exercise, we'll create hexagons on what seems like a very odd-sized block. You can create accurate templates, foundation patterns, or play with colors and fabrics in EQ5!

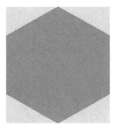 

Vertical Hexagon   *Horizontal Hexagon*

We'll start by drawing a base block for hexagons. We'll keep the math simple and only use what we need to create a quilt block!

1 On the BLOCK menu, point to New Block, click EasyDraw™. Turn Snap to Grid ON, Snap to Node ON, Snap to Drawing OFF.

2 Also on the BLOCK menu, click Drawing Board Setup and enter these values:

General Tab
Snap to Grid Points
    Horizontal = 24   Vertical = 24
Block Size
    Horizontal = 6   Vertical = 6.93
Graph Paper Tab
Number of Divisions
    Horizontal = 4   Vertical = 4
Options
    Style = Graph paper lines

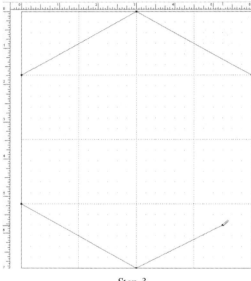

Step 3

> ⎰**Tip** ————————————————
> • **Yes, you can indeed type this odd number in the Block Size box. Trust me on the size for now and later on we'll discuss why.**

3 Click on the Line tool. Draw a line from the top center of the block to the first graph paper line down from the top left. Draw a second line beginning at top center to the same graph paper line on the right side of the block. Draw a mirror image of these lines at the bottom of the block.

4

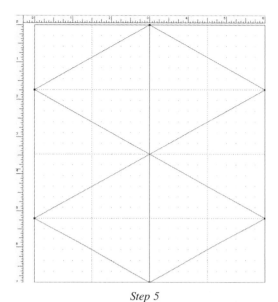

Step 5

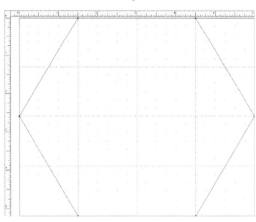

Step 8

Tada! Now you have a nicely proportioned hexagonal block, or maybe we should say a hexagon in a rectangle.

4   Save this block in the Sketchbook.

Let's divide the hexagon into equilateral triangles now (i.e. triangles with all sides equal) and then have a very painless discussion about the geometry of a hexagon.

5   Draw lines across the hexagon from point to point, dividing it into six equilateral triangles as illustrated.

6   Save in Sketchbook.

Notice that we've created the block with the parallel flat sides of the hexagon on the left and right of the block (referred to as a vertical hexagon). You can also draw it with the flat sides at top and bottom (a horizontal hexagon) by switching the horizontal and vertical block size in the Drawing Board Setup. Now, let's draw a horizontal hexagon too.

Drawing a Horizontal Hexagon

7   On the BLOCK menu, point to New Block, click EasyDraw™. Turn Snap to Grid ON, Snap to Node ON, Snap to Drawing OFF.

8   In Drawing Board Setup, *change the Block Size to 6.00" horizontal and 5.19" vertical.* All other settings should not be changed. Draw lines from the center of the sides to the first graph paper lines in from each side as illustrated.

9   Save this block in the Sketchbook. Also take a moment and save the two base hexagon blocks in the User Libraries. We're going to use them a lot in the next exercises!

4

How to calculate a hexagon's size

Now for that painless geometry I mentioned. The most important thing to remember about a hexagonal block is its proportions. *The ratio of a hexagon from its shortest measurement across (flat side to flat side) to its longest measurement (point to point) is 1 to 1.155.*

Remember this: 1 to 1.155

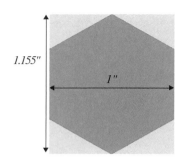

You will need to remember this ratio when drawing hexagon blocks from scratch and when adding in the size for a quilt layout. It's *very* important when you print the block!

Any multiple of 4 can be used for the Snap to Grid points. We used 24 x 24 because it's divisible by more numbers (2, 3, 4, 6, 8…). If you need to divide the sides of a hexagon by a number that does not divide into 24, multiply the number of segments you need by 4 and then change the Snap to Grid points in the Drawing Board Setup accordingly. For example, if you need to divide the sides into 5 segments, use 20 (5 x 4 = 20).

Take a look at the hexagonal block we divided into equilateral triangles. *The distance between two points of a hexagon is equal to twice the length of its sides.* Therefore, if you want the measurement of the sides to be a whole number (as opposed to hundredths of an inch), *keep the point to point measurement a whole number.* The same is true for a horizontal hexagon.

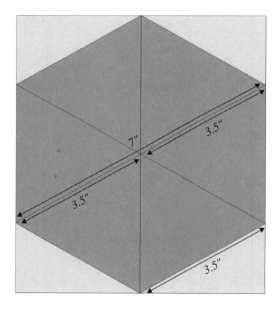

You will also find it helpful to make the snap points a multiple of the whole number. This will keep the grid divisions along flat sides easily divisible. For example, if your block is 6.93" x 6.00" make the snap points 24 x 24, not 20 x 20.

If you want the measurement from flat side to flat side to be a whole number, the sides of your hexagon will be figured in hundredths of an inch size – which is fine, as long as it suits the purpose of your quilt design!

4

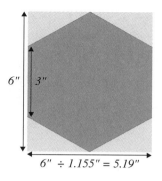

Example 1

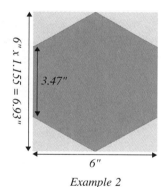

Example 2

Here are a couple of examples:

- If the height of a vertical hexagon is 6", the sides will all be 3". To determine the width of the hexagon, divide the height by 1.155. Round up the resulting width to two decimal points.

  6" ÷ 1.155 = 5.19"

  The block size would be 6" x 5.19".

- If you want the width of the vertical hexagon to be 6", multiply the width times 1.155.

  6" x 1.155 = 6.93"

  The block size would be 6" x 6.93" and the sides of the hexagon will measure 3.47".

In a quilt layout, you will need to find the closest number possible when setting the block size. The block size in quilt layouts by default is set in 1/4" increments.

Tip

- In EQ5, we can change the size increments for block size in quilt layouts down to 1/32 of an inch. If you want more precise hexagonal blocks in the quilt layout, go to the FILE menu, Preferences, Layout Options tab. Under Nudge Settings, change the fractions to a smaller size.

Review

Let's recap the important points to remember about designing hexagonal blocks:

- The ratio of a hexagon from its shortest measurement across (flat side to flat side) to its longest measurement (point to point) is 1 to 1.155.

- The distance between two points of a hexagon is equal to twice the length of its sides.

- Keep the point to point measurement a whole number for ease of designing, cutting, and sewing.

4

Hexagons Cubed

Try these three cube blocks on your vertical hexagon base block.

Variation 1 – Plain Cube

Use the base block saved in Step 6 (page 207). Delete three of the lines so that you create three 60° diamonds.

Variation 2 – Four Patch Cube

Use the block created in Variation 1. Partition the hexagon sides inside the block in half. Draw lines to create a diamond four patch within each of the three diamonds.

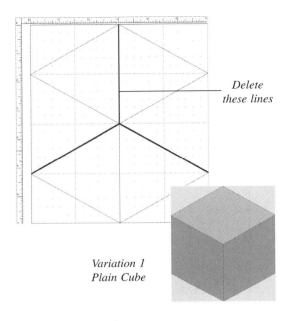

Delete these lines

Variation 1
Plain Cube

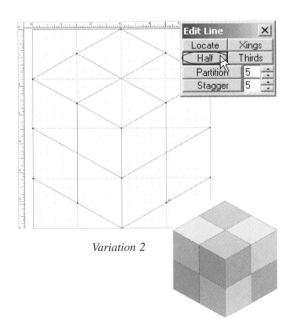

Variation 2

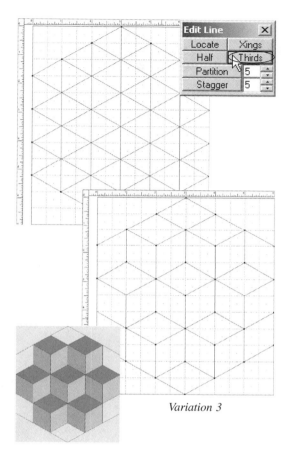

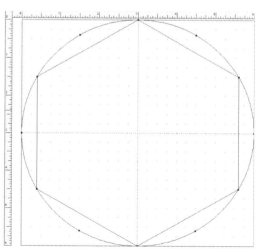

Variation 3

Variation 3 – Flower Cube

Start with the base vertical hexagon. Partition the hexagon sides inside the block into thirds. In Drawing Board Setup, change the vertical Graph Paper lines to 12, so you can easily see where to park the lines along the block sides.

Draw a triangular grid as illustrated (no horizontal lines). Save your block in the Sketchbook to create nodes. Using the block picture as your guide, delete lines in some of the diamonds to create the Flower Cube.

Another way to draw hexagons

You may already be familiar with another way to create a hexagon in a square block in EasyDraw™. Draw a circle, partition the arcs in thirds, and draw lines between every other node. Delete the arcs after the hexagon is drawn.

This method will give you very accurate templates, but it cannot be used in a quilt layout, therefore I will let you experiment with it on your own. Most of the blocks in the next two exercises can also be drawn on this "hexagon in a square" block. I felt it was important to mention it in case you want to try this method too.

4

Drawing Hexagonal Stars

*Color blocks
on page 175 – 176*

There are so many possibilities with hexagonal stars. It's hard knowing where to begin! We'll start with a basic star, then work through a few variations.

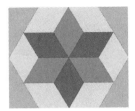

Hexagonal Star

1 Retrieve the horizontal hexagon block from the exercise, *Drawing a Base for Hexagonal Blocks* on page 206 and place it on the worktable. If you have not worked through the previous exercise, you will need to complete it before continuing with this one. (You can also draw a new one if you like.)

Turn Snap to Grid ON, Snap to Node ON, Snap to Drawing OFF. In the Drawing Board Setup, the settings are the same as for the horizontal hexagon:

General Tab

Snap to Grid Points

Horizontal = 24   Vertical = 24

Block Size

Horizontal = 6   Vertical = 5.19

Graph Paper Tab

Number of Divisions

Horizontal = 4   Vertical = 4

Options

Style = Graph paper lines

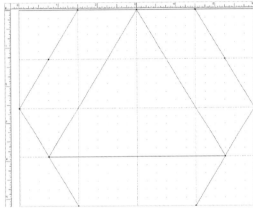

Step 4

2 Click on the small black square in the corner of the Edit tool, to open the Edit Line box.

3 Click on each of the hexagon's four lines within the block, and then on the Edit Line box, click on Half.

4 Click on the Line tool. Draw an upright triangle within the hexagon with the top point at the top center and the bottom points at the side nodes on the bottom half of the hexagon (nodes at 12 o'clock, 4 o'clock, and 8 o'clock).

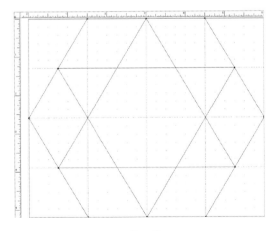

Step 5

4

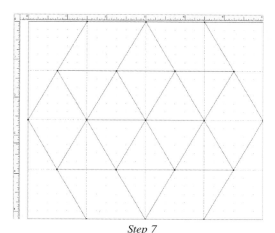

Step 7

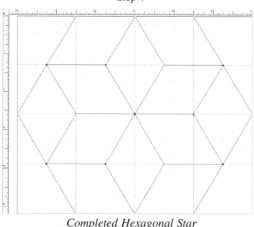

Completed Hexagonal Star

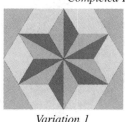

Variation 1

Variation 2

Variation 3

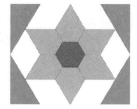

Variation 4

5 Draw a second triangle in the opposite direction (nodes at 6 o'clock, 10 o'clock and 2 o'clock).

6 Save in Sketchbook to establish nodes.

7 Draw three diagonal lines from point to point inside the hexagonal center of the star, as illustrated.

8 Save in Sketchbook again.

9 Click on the Select tool and delete the lines that make up the center hexagon. You should have a star made up of six 60° diamonds.

10 Save your new hexagonal star in the Sketchbook.

Hexagonal Star Variations

These hexagonal star variations are all traditional blocks drawn on the horizontal hexagon base. Drawing these will help you learn how you can divide up a hexagon in EasyDraw™.

Variation 1 – Star of the East
Use the star saved in Step 10. Draw lines across the block from point to point dividing each diamond in half.

Variation 2 – Glistening Star
Use the star saved in Step 10. Partition each line of the hexagonal star into thirds, draw lines to create a diamond Nine Patch in each point.

Variation 3 – Hexagon Beauty Star
Use the star saved in Step 8. Partition each line inside the center hexagon in half. Draw lines from the new nodes to create another hexagon in the center of the star.

Variation 4 – Texas Star
Use the star saved in Variation 3. Delete the lines of the second largest hexagon as well as the lines on the inside of the smallest hexagon.

4

Variation 5 – Ozark Diamonds

Use the star saved in Step 6. Partition, in half, each line that forms the triangle star points. Draw two lines to complete diamonds in the points. Then draw two opposite triangles to create the star in the center.

Variation 6 – Mountain Star

Use the Ozark Diamonds above. Create the center star in the same manner as the plain Hexagonal Star block in the first part of this exercise.

Variation 5   *Variation 6*

Tip

- You can also draw these stars with the star points in the points of the hexagon! Use the vertical hexagon block if you want the star points at the top and bottom. If you draw your stars this way, the background shapes around the star will be half-diamonds.

- Remember to save your blocks in the User Libraries!

On-point Star
Draw the star points in the points
of a vertical hexagon block.

Using the blocks in a Strip Quilt

Make a sampler quilt of your hexagonal star blocks! For horizontal hexagons, use the Horizontal Strip quilt layout, for vertical hexagons, use the Vertical Strip. You can also rotate the blocks in either style strip quilt; it all depends on how you want your blocks oriented in the quilt.

When you alternate the strips as instructed on the next page (215), a secondary star is formed around the central hexagon. If you were to make this quilt, you would want these to be one-piece triangles. You can calculate the size of the triangles easily if you know the measurement of your hexagon's side — remember the sides are all equal on an equilateral triangle!

Strip Quilt Layout

4

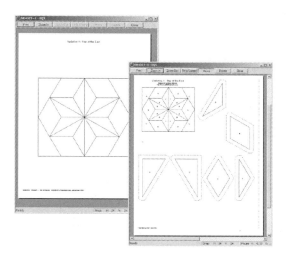

Print the blocks, templates, and foundation patterns to ensure accurate size and angles.

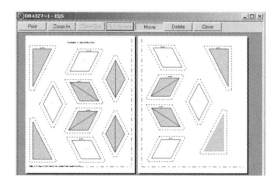

Tip

- See pages 34 – 37 of the *EQ5 Design Cookbook* for more information about the Strip Quilt layouts. Also, check out strip quilts in the Online Help files under Designing a Quilt, Choosing a Layout. You will see even more help with the math!

Here are the settings for the quilt illustrated.

Block Size – 10" x 8.66".

Total Strips – 3

Strip Styles – Going from top to bottom, alternate Half Drop and Pieced Blocks

Strip Width – 8.66" or the height of your block. Note: You can get exactly 8.66" if you change the Nudge settings to 1/32" in Preferences. Otherwise, just use 8.50" or 8.75" so you can play with colorings on the quilt.

Strip Length – 30.00" or 3 x the width of your block.

Number of blocks across – 3

Tip

- I recommend printing the blocks, templates, foundation patterns, or rotary cutting directions from the Block Worktable to ensure size and angle accuracy.

4

Drawing a Seven Sisters Block

Color block on page 176

Let's try a hexagonal block that has 5 divisions along the sides. This Seven Sisters block is made up of seven hexagonal stars.

1   Retrieve the horizontal hexagon block from the exercise, *Drawing a Base for Hexagonal Blocks* on page 206 and place it on the worktable. If you have not worked through the two previous exercises, I highly recommend that you do them before continuing with this one. (You can also draw a new one if you like.)

Turn Snap to Grid ON, Snap to Node ON, Snap to Drawing OFF. Since this block has five divisions along the sides, we will need to change the Drawing Board Setup to match that.

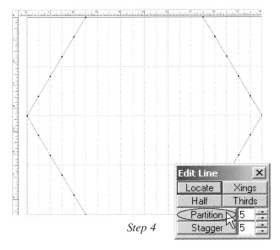

Step 4

2   In the Drawing Board Setup, enter these values:

   General Tab
   Snap to Grid Points
       Horizontal = 20   Vertical = 20
   Block Size
       Horizontal = 10   Vertical = 8.66
   Graph Paper Tab
   Number of Divisions
       Horizontal = 20 Vertical = 4
   Options
       Style = Graph paper lines

3   Click on the small black square in the corner of the Edit tool to open the Edit Line box.

4   On the Edit Line box, make sure that the Partition number is 5. Then, click on each hexagon side within the block and click on Partition.

5   Click on the Line tool.

6   Draw a triangular grid within the hexagon as illustrated. There are no vertical lines. Every two vertical graph paper divisions represent one segment.

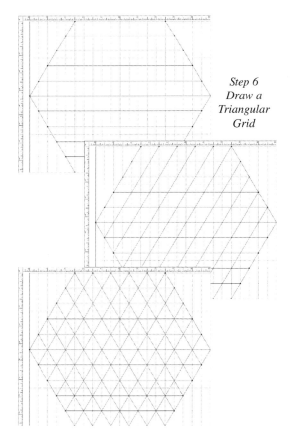

*Step 6
Draw a
Triangular
Grid*

4

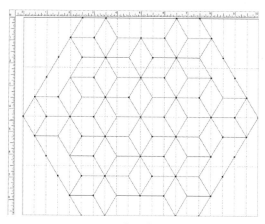

Step 8

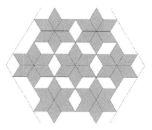

Completed Seven Sisters Block

Variation 1

Variation 2

7   Save in the Sketchbook to establish nodes.

The next step reminds me of those find-the-hidden-object games! Locate the seven stars using the completed block illustration as your guide. Each star is made up of diamonds just like the basic hexagonal star.

8   Click on the Select tool. Using the completed block picture as your guide, delete the lines between the seven stars. Also delete the lines within the stars that divide the star point diamonds in half.

You may find it helpful to start at the top of the block and work your way down. If you accidentally delete the wrong lines, you can easily redraw them.

9   When you are finished deleting the lines, save the block in the Sketchbook. You will probably want to color it at this point too, so you can admire your handiwork!

So remember…dividing a hexagon into a triangle grid is the most accurate way to draw a hexagonal block with odd numbered divisions.

Try this: Place the gridded block saved in Step 7 back on the worktable. See what other designs you can create by deleting lines. If it helps, print it out and get your colored pencils! Here are two blocks that I found.

4

Drawing 60° Log Cabins & Pineapples

Color blocks on page 176

If you like square Pineapple and Log Cabin blocks, try your drawing skills on these hexagonal ones!

It's interesting that Log Cabin hexagons look a lot like what we know as Pineapple blocks (the square ones). Square Log Cabin blocks are made up of squares and rectangular logs. Square Pineapples are made up of triangles and elongated trapezoids. Since the hexagon doesn't have right-angled corners, this is what we get. So…when does a Pineapple become a Log Cabin? When it's a hexagon, of course!

Log Cabin Hexagon Block

We'll start with a basic "four log" block. Once you learn how, you can make as many logs in your block as you like!

1   Retrieve the horizontal hexagon block from the exercise, *Drawing a Base for Hexagonal Blocks* on page 206 and place it on the worktable. Turn Snap to Grid ON, Snap to Node ON, Snap to Drawing OFF.

2   In the Drawing Board Setup, enter these values:

General Tab
Snap to Grid Points
     Horizontal = 20   Vertical = 20
Block Size
     Horizontal = 10   Vertical = 8.66
Graph Paper Tab
Number of Divisions
     Horizontal = 20   Vertical = 20
Options
     Style = Graph paper lines

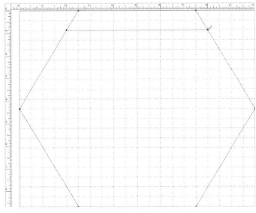

Step 4

With this setup, we can draw the logs without partitioning any lines. The graph paper lines will show you exactly where to draw.

3   Click on the Line tool.

4   Beginning at the top, draw the first line across the hexagon on the second graph paper line down from the top of the block.

Try these three variations of the same Log
Cabin Hexagon block. All three can be drawn
with just a few added lines – no deleting or
partitioning necessary! I think that last one
looks like a Pineapple block, don't you?

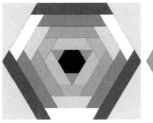

Log Cabin Hexagon Block   *Variation 1*

Pineapple Geese?

Here is an original block for you to try. It falls
into the same category as Pineapples and Log
Cabins... but is it a Pineapple? It looks more
like Flying Geese to me, so I have dubbed it,
"Pineapple Geese."

1   Retrieve the horizontal hexagon block
    from the exercise, *Drawing a Base for
    Hexagonal Blocks* on page 206 and place it
    on the worktable. Turn Snap to Grid ON,
    Snap to Node ON, Snap to Drawing OFF.

Variation 2   *Variation 3*

2   In the Drawing Board Setup, enter these
    values:

    General Tab
    Snap to Grid Points
        Horizontal = 24   Vertical = 24
    Block Size
        Horizontal = 6   Vertical = 5.19
    Graph Paper Tab
    Number of Divisions
        Horizontal = 4   Vertical = 4
    Options
        Style = Graph paper lines

3   Click on the small black square in the
    corner of the Edit tool to open the Edit
    Line box.

4   Click on each side of the hexagon within
    the block and on the Edit Line box click on
    Half.

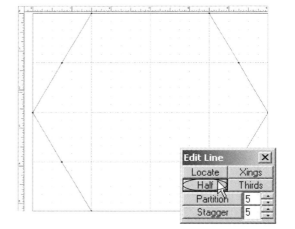

4

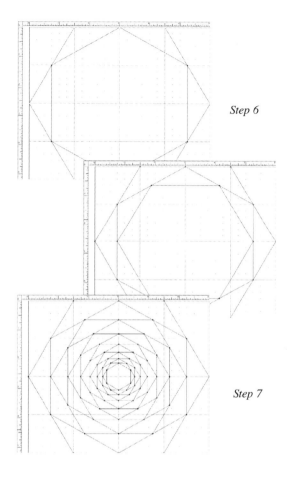

Step 6

Step 7

5 Click on the Line tool.

6 Draw a vertical hexagon within the base hexagon beginning at the top center and using the nodes that were just added.

7 Click on the small black square in the corner of the Edit tool to open the Edit Line box. Partition each side of the new hexagon in half. Then, draw another hexagon using these new nodes. Repeat this step until you have 13 hexagons (14 total) inside the base hexagon. The small center hexagon will be vertical.

If you lose track of the number of hexagons, it's okay. Instead, count the triangles down from the top center. There should be six of them.

Did I mention you can make a foundation pattern for this block? Take a look at the numbering!

Take time to set this block in a Strip Quilt layout as instructed on page 214, under *Using the Blocks in a Strip Quilt*. Color the blocks in black and white and use a black background. The resulting effect is pretty cool! Can you see the snowflake?

Completed Pineapple Geese Block

Pineapple Geese in a Strip Quilt Layout

4

60° Blocks in PatchDraw

We've learned a lot about how to draw hexagons in EasyDraw™. But now we're going to build one with closed shapes in PatchDraw. Sometimes you want your hexagon blocks to be...well...hexagons! When we're done, we'll have a free floating hexagonal motif to play with in the Custom Set quilt layout or on Layer 2.

60° Ozark Motif

⟋ Tip ————————————————

- **If you have not worked through the exercise on *Drawing Hexagonal Stars* on page 212, you will need to complete it before continuing with this lesson. You will need one or more of the hexagonal star variations to use in this exercise.**

1   Retrieve the hexagonal star variation, Ozark Diamonds, from the Sketchbook or User Library and place it on the worktable.

2   Click on the Color tab and color the block with pale solid colors to make it easy to trace. Use at least two colors for good contrast. We're going to export it as a bitmap and then import it back into PatchDraw for tracing.

Ozark Diamonds Block

3   Follow the directions for "Getting the Picture" on page 162, and export a snapshot of the pale colored Ozark Diamonds block and save it as a Windows bitmap. Be sure to remember where you saved it!

⟋ Tip ————————————————

- **You could also use an Overlaid block to accomplish this hexagonal block in PatchDraw. However, it's much harder to see where to place the shapes. Using an imported bitmap has three advantages you will find very helpful. One, you can turn the bitmap on and off to keep track as you build your block. Two, when you have a pale colored bitmap under the drawing board, the grid dots are much easier to see. And three, when you're done, you don't have to worry about copying and pasting the appliqué layer onto a new PatchDraw block!**

4   On BLOCK menu, point to New Block, click on PatchDraw.

4

Step 6

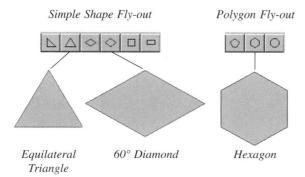

Step 7

Simple Shape Fly-out   *Polygon Fly-out*

Equilateral   *60° Diamond*   *Hexagon*
Triangle

5   In the Drawing Board Setup, enter these values:

General Tab
Snap to Grid Points
    Horizontal = 48   Vertical = 48
Block Size
    Horizontal = 6   Vertical = 5.19
Graph Paper Tab
Number of Divisions
    Horizontal = 12   Vertical = 12
Options
    Style = Graph paper lines

6   On the BLOCK menu, click on Import for Tracing. Navigate to where you saved the Ozark Diamonds bitmap, select it, then click on Open to place the bitmap on the drawing board. When you import a bitmap, you will automatically be on the bitmap tab. Adjust the bitmap so that it is centered on the block worktable.

7   Click on the PatchDraw tab.

If you were careful about capturing your EasyDraw™ block, the image should fit perfectly underneath the PatchDraw drawing board and you'll be ready to move on to the next step. If the image is just a little off, don't worry about it. All of the shapes are going to snap into place anyway!

We're going to build this entire hexagonal block using only three pre-closed shapes! Two of them, the equilateral triangle and the 60° diamond, are on the Simple Shape tool fly-out. We'll also use the hexagon from the Polygon tool fly-out. You should already be familiar with using these tools, so I will only tell you when and where to place them.

4

8 We'll need some help getting our shapes into place, so ***turn ON all of the Advanced Drawing features…*** Snap to Grid, Snap to Node, Auto Align Similar Lines, and Snap Patch to Grid.

Step 8
All Snap Tools
turned ON

Now we are ready to begin!

9 Using the hexagon shape, and going from the center point on the left side to the center point on the right side, trace the large base hexagon. Since Snap to Grid is on and our block is proportional, the hexagon will be perfectly placed, fitting neatly in the block.

10 Now, click on the Select tool, select the square block outline and delete it – we don't need it anymore!

11 Using the 60° diamond tool, trace all six of the larger background diamonds. Snap to Grid makes this so easy!

12 Save the block at this stage in the Sketchbook. You can use it later for the other hexagonal stars!

Optional step: Once you have the hexagon block defined by placing shapes within it, you can delete the large base hexagon. Move one of the diamonds over a little so that you can select the hexagon and delete it. Move the diamond back into place when you are done. Doing this gives you another way to check if you missed tracing any of the shapes. Click on the Color tab and use the Spraycan tool to fill the block with color. If you missed a shape, it will show!

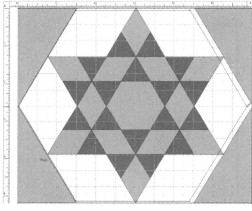

Step 9

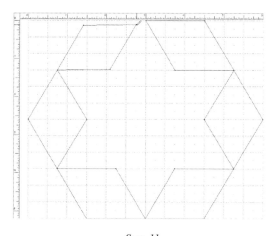

Step 11

4

Hide/Show Bitmap Tool

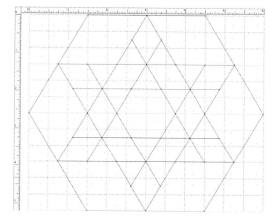

Steps 14 & 15

Completed Ozark Mountains Motif

13 Still using the 60° diamond shape, trace the vertical diamond in the top-center star point. Click on the equilateral triangle tool and trace the triangles in the star point.

14 Trace the diamonds and triangles in the other five star points.

There are other ways to repeat the shapes in the star points. You can clone all three shapes together and rotate them 60° degrees using the Rotate option on the right-click context menu. However, you may find it quicker to just trace each shape separately. Try both methods and decide which you like best.

15 Once you have the shapes in all six star points, trace the remaining shapes in the center of the block, tracing the center hexagon last.

16 Check once more to make sure you have traced all the pieces of this hexagon puzzle, then save your new free-floating Ozark Diamonds in the Sketchbook. Since you deleted the block outline, this block will be saved on the motifs tab in the Sketchbook.

4

Now that you've recreated one of your star variations, why not try some others?

Creating those "other" 60° shapes

Some hexagonal blocks have odd shapes not included on those handy fly-out menus. Let me show you how to use the features on the Edit Arc pop-up box to create them from the pre-closed shapes we have available. Once you learn the process, you will need to make the shapes conform to the size needed for your particular block.

On the BLOCK menu, point to New Block, Click PatchDraw.

Tip
- **If you need to delete the Bitmap in the background, first make sure you are on the Bitmap tab. Then, right-click on the picture and click Delete.**

For each procedure below, when you click on the Edit tool, click on the small black square in the corner to open the Edit Arc box.

Half-Diamonds
Draw a 60° diamond. Using the Edit tool, click on the node on the long side of the diamond, then click Delete on the Edit Arc box.

Gems
Draw a 60° diamond. Using the Edit tool, click on one side of the diamond, then click Add on the Edit Arc box. A node will be added to the center of the line. Repeat on the opposite side. Delete the node at the tip.

Kites (a.k.a. teardrops)
Draw a hexagon. Delete two opposite nodes on the parallel flat sides of the hexagon.

Trapezoids
Draw a hexagon. Delete two nodes on the same flat side.

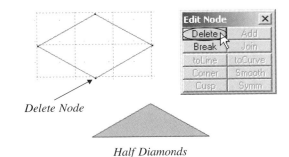

Delete Node

Half Diamonds

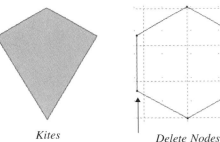

Delete Node

Add Node   *Add Node*

Gems

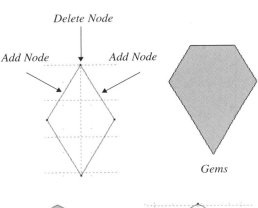

Kites

Delete Nodes

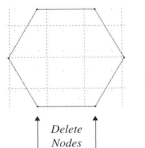

Trapezoids

Delete Nodes

4

Hexagon Quilt Layout

These are some of the most common shapes you will need to create hexagonal designs. If you need a shape not included here, first try to use one of the pre-closed shapes to create it. If that won't work, draw it with the Line tool.

Tip

- If you are working on a block and some of the patches do not fall on the grid, try setting as many adjacent shapes as possible around the area first where they need to go. This will create a space that will give the patch something to snap to.

Math help for hexagon quilt layouts

Need help laying out your hexagon motif quilt? Try placing your blocks on Layer 2 of one of the One Patch hexagon quilt layouts. When you click on the layout tab, you will see there's a horizontal and a vertical hexagon patch style. In the Hexagon [H] patch style for example, if you total the numbers in the boxes above the hexagon preview, that is your measurement from point to point. The good news is that these layouts will also help you with the math!

Seven of these star hexagons will make a *really* nice quilt don't you think?

4

Index

Index

Tools *Quick Reference*

EQ5 Tools *Quick Reference*

Project Tools

 Create a New Project

 Open a Project

 Save

 Print

 Export Snapshot

Export Metafile

 View Sketchbook

 Save in Sketchbook

 Zoom In

 Zoom Out

 Refresh Screen

Fit to Window

Edit Tools

 Cut

 Copy

 Paste

Quilt Tools

 Select tool

 Adjust tool

Tape Measure tool

 Set tool

Plain Block tool

 Rotate tool

Flip tool

Symmetry tool

Color Tools

 Paintbrush tool

Spraycan tool

 Swap tool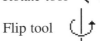

Thread Color tool

Eyedropper tool

Fussy Cut tool

EQ4 Spraycan tool

EQ4 Swap tool

EasyDraw™/ Pieced Tools

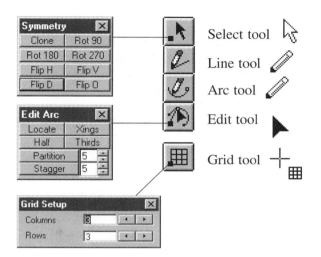

Select tool

Line tool

Arc tool

Edit tool

Grid tool

Advanced EasyDraw™ Tools

Snap to Grid

Snap to Node

Snap to Drawing

Hide/Show Graph Paper

Advanced PatchDraw Tools

Snap to Grid

Snap to Node

Snap Patch to Grid

Hide/Show Graph Paper

Auto Align Similar Lines

To see these advanced tools on your screen, see: Adding the Advanced Drawing Features (pg 76-77).

PatchDraw / Appliqué Tools

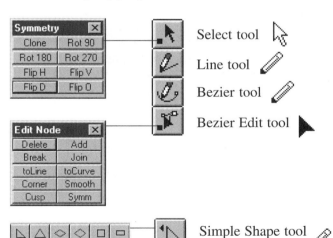

Select tool

Line tool

Bezier tool

Bezier Edit tool

Simple Shape tool

Polygon tool

Simple Oval tool

Tracing Tools

Resize tool

Crop tool

Hide/Show Bitmap

About the Author

Patti R. Anderson is a professional quiltmaker, quilt teacher, and pattern designer from West Virginia. She currently teaches the advanced and feature-specific EQ classes at QuiltUniversity.com, as well as several other quilt making classes.

Several years ago, Patti launched her website, www.patchpieces.com, with the goal of getting her work known in the quilting world. She regularly puts free EQ lessons in her "EQ Patch," to demonstrate to other users how to tap its full potential. She has become quite well known for stretching the limits of EQ beyond the obvious, and often beta tests new software for the Electric Quilt Company.

Patti has been sewing since she was nine years old and quilt-making for over 15 years. She spent her first years as a quiltmaker making and selling her quilts and quilted products on consignment and in several craft shops around the state under the name Patchpieces. Patti no longer sells her quilts, but now teaches others how to make and design them.

Patti lives in Shinnston, West Virginia with her husband Robert, who is a United Methodist pastor. They have two lovely, talented daughters; Naomi, who finished college as an English/Writing major about the same time as this book was published, and Bethany, who is a sophomore Physics major (who thinks she may be in college forever). Also living in the Anderson household are Rascal, their 13 year old cat, and Grommit, the cutest Husky-mutt you ever saw.